GREAT NORTHERN
COOKBOOK

SANDY'S GREAT NORTHERN COOKBOOK

Scran for Every Occasion

Sandy Docherty

Scratching Shed Publishing Ltd

Typeset in Warnock Pro Semi Bold and Palatino
Printed and bound in the United Kingdom by
Page Bros (Norwich) Ltd
Mile Cross Lane, Norwich, Norfolk NR6 6SA
Telephone 01603 778800

Page
Bros
Group

For Mum

Contents

Foreword

FOOD IS SUCH an important unifier of communities and people. It evokes memories of our childhood and provides comfort, security and a feeling of all being well in the world.

It reinforces our sense of belonging and preserves many different traditions, which have been lovingly passed down from generation to generation.

Yorkshire is bursting with many cherished recipes influenced both by its own history and the many diverse communities that live in the county and have made it their home. During the Covid pandemic, we all learned the true value of family and friends as we missed shared mealtimes and special occasions with those we love.

By baking, cooking and eating together again, we have reconnected and learned never to take such simple pleasures for granted.

Sandy has brilliantly captured this sentiment in her cookbook. It has clearly been a labour of love for her, as well as a celebration of food and the people that create it.

Such is her talent for cooking and storytelling, you can almost smell and taste the recipes off the page – and easily imagine the people and conversations she had with them on her various travels.

This is a cookbook to treasure, whose recipes it should be a pleasure to follow and pass on.

Nicky Chance Thompson
CEO The Piece Hall Trust

Introduction

WHAT AN ADVENTURE it has been, since my days on the *Great British Bake Off*. I would never have envisaged being able to stand up and demonstrate baking in front of hundreds of people, give talks on my passion to Women's Institute groups, or working closely with the Help for Heroes Phoenix House recovery centre, while contributing to so many other organisations and charities.

One of the high spots has been able to make cakes for the 200th birthday commemorations of the Brontë sisters, Emily, Charlotte and Anne, and also their father Patrick. I was even mentioned in the newspapers, together with the patron of the Brontës Society Dame Judy Dench – me and Judy in the same sentence!

Through *GBBO* I've met some of the most tremendous people. And working in the events industry has allowed me to travel the country alongside folk with an infectious sense of fun and an incredible work ethic. Danny and Janine from

Great British Food Festival, Glyn and Katie from Wots Cooking – you all taught me to believe in myself and gave me scope to 'perform'.

The places and people I have encountered on my post *Bake Off* trail have all been so uplifting, like the artisan traders and crafts people of Ludlow Food Festival, passionate about what they make. This country is full of small independents that live and breathe their work. Seek them out and buy their goods – you will have supported something most often unique that maintains a tradition and pays back.

To bring it home, the pride at being asked to work with Lotherton Hall, on the outskirts of Leeds, on Yorkshire Day; to be invited to Wensleydale Creamery; to work closely with Bradford and Leeds Hospitals – all reinforced how important the north is for food and the traditions associated with it.

This book has been a joy to write, not least because chronicling these recipes for the region will, hopefully, see them passed down to another generation.

Creating them and linking them to people, places, organisations and landmarks from the north of England has been an absolute pleasure.

Cooking and baking are the very essences of who I am. They share a universal language that crosses worlds. In all cultures, food speaks. Whether it is about making the best of what is available or creating abundance, universally it says 'please share.'

But, for myself, the ultimate reason to bake and cook is to say, 'I love and care about you.'

Recently, we have all been unable to embrace or get too close to people we care about and, as we have seen on so many levels, sharing food is the culinary equivalent of a hug.

Some of the recipes and stories here reflect my family, who are the most important thing to me. To share and adapt some of my mum's old recipes has been a real pull. Revisiting her hand-written notes has been an emotional journey of tears and laughter and the occasional time when I have looked up to heaven and said, 'How much is *some* mum?'

And then, somehow, she has given me the answer.

Mum was always with me on my adventures through *Bake Off*. She loved the trips to London, to advise me on my bakes, always ready to wash up when I was practising. In fact, if it wasn't for Mum pushing me forward for it, *Bake Off* would never have happened – therefore I dedicate this book to her.

Mum and dad believed in me when I had very little confidence. I struggled throughout my teenage years and young adulthood to find some self-worth; baking became my outlet.

My sister is an inspiration too. Never a day goes by when she has not boosted me in some way, while my brothers have been the font of constructive criticism as only brothers can say it. My son may not have got around to putting up that kitchen shelf yet, but he gave me the most precious gift of a grandson, while Tom, my man, is always there with a cup of tea or something stronger.

Finally, Scratching Shed Publishing have my gratitude for encouraging me to challenge myself with these new and exciting recipes that reflect the north of England – the perfect marriage of my favourite foods with my favourite places.

I hope you enjoy cooking the recipes and eating the results. I bring them to you from my heart and that of my mum. Please keep sharing and always remember that food can say so much.

Sandy xx

1

'SUMMAT TO BE GOING ON WI'

A term used to describe food that can be eaten as soon as possible.
Alternatively, a light snack or starter size.

ADEL PIES

LEEDS SOUP

MENWITH CHEESE CAKES

MRS WHYMES' SINGING HINNIES

OUT OF THE BOX SCONE

SUNDRIED TOMATO AND FETA SCONES

SWALEDALE LAMB AND MINT PIES

THE DALES CRACKER

THE GROWLER

Adel Pies

ADEL PIES

Tucked away in the corner of a small, otherwise unobtrusive cul de sac in Adel, north Leeds, is a dairy producing some of the finest continental cheeses in the whole of Yorkshire.

Mario Olianas came from Sardinia to learn English and he settled in Yorkshire.

All his produce is made with sheeps' milk and produced to the highest standard. You can find him at farmers markets in and around West Yorkshire, where you can purchase pecorino, feta and halloumi-style cheeses, among his other continental foods.

These pies are easy to make

but so very tasty. You can style them vegan but using all white vegetable fat in the pastry and leaving out the feta from the filling.

Pastry

Follow the Best Northern Short Crust Pastry recipe in part 5, but replace the flour with sun dried tomato flour.

If you can't get hold of that, add a good tablespoon of sundried tomato paste to the water or mix in with the flour (this will make it a bit clumpy when rubbing in, but it will be fine when the pastry is kneaded).
Pre-heated oven: Gas 4, 350f, 180c, 160 fan

Ingredients

1 courgette;
1 aubergine;
1 red onion;
1 pepper (red, green or yellow);
4 cloves of garlic crushed;
1 tin of chopped tomatoes;
½ tube of tomato puree;
salt and pepper;
1 teaspoon of dried herbs (oregano is best);
250g feta cheese;
egg or water to glaze

Method

Chop everything except the feta into bite-size chunks, (remember if you make your pies small you need to be able to have a mixture of veg in each pie).

I find that using a slow cooker is good for this filling. Fill it or an oven-proof casserole with the chopped vegetables, tinned tomatoes, puree and crushed garlic, season well and sprinkle on the herbs (dried are good as they have a more intense flavour) in a moderate oven, so that the

veg does not dry out, or on high in the slow cooker.

The veg will become very soft and well amalgamated.

It's important to keep tasting the ratatouille as more salt and pepper could be needed. It never harms to drop in a glug of red wine, to assist with the flavour.

Once cooked to perfection, leave to cool completely. This may be better done in advance, the day before you need to make the pies.

Chop the feta and stir into the veg mixture. For an added hit, you can double the cheese amount. Line each tart tin with a disc of pastry and pack with a good dessert spoon of filling, brush the lid or second circle with egg and lay over the filling and bottom circle. Crimp the edges together making sure they stick.

Make a small knife incision in the top of each pie, brush with egg, and bake in a pre-heated oven for about 35-40 minutes.

If making vegan pies, use water to stick the pastry together.

Cool in the tin slightly before removing carefully and allow your pies to cool completely.

Leeds Soup

LEEDS SOUP

Leeds, a truly cosmopolitan city of diversity and colour, also has Kirkgate market – a fascinating place full of culture, embracing produce from around the word.

Traders touting for your business offer great deals on fruit, vegetables, fish and bread, plus spices, cheese and fresh flowers.

As much as this soup is based on the traditional minestrone, it is also very dependent on the mix of races, colours and creeds that Leeds celebrates.

I make it in large batches, which is great to freeze, but also lunch for a large family group – when you get them round to help you garden or decorate and they want feeding as part of the deal!

The amounts will give you about three pints of soup in total. You will need a large stock pot style pan.

Ingredients

200g diced smoked bacon (optional); 2 tablespoons oil; 1 large onion finely chopped; 2 sticks finely chopped celery; 1 large carrot finely diced; 1 leek finely sliced; 2 tins of chopped tomatoes; ½ tube of tomato puree; 1 carton of pasata (sieved tomatoes bit like tomato juice just thicker); 2 teaspoons of sugar; 2 cloves crushed garlic; ½ teaspoon crushed chillies (optional); 2 tins of cannellini beans, butter beans or haricot beans (tins/jars of beans are soft, creamy and convenient. I sometimes mix up the beans and use a tin of black beans or kidney beans; 2 vegetable or chicken stock cubes (jellied type); 1 glass red wine (optional); 150g dried uncooked spaghetti; salt and pepper; chopped parsley or mixed herbs

7

Method

Take some time to chop the veg small. This soup is not liquidised, so relies on all parts being the correct size from the off.

In a large stock pot pan, fry the bacon so it releases some of its flavour and oil.

If you are not using bacon, then heat up the oil.

Sauté the diced veg, including the onion, in the bacon/oil for just a couple of minutes until the vegetables are coated. Add in the crushed garlic and crushed chilli – with the chilli you can always use less, it's worth just a touch to add another flavour dimension.

Put in the tomatoes, the stock cube and the pasata and give everything a good stir. Add the sugar, (which cuts the acidity of tomatoes, but leave it out if you wish) add in the puree. It's worth tasting at this stage it will probably need salt. Add salt and pepper and the wine, plus about 300mls of water,

allow the soup to simmer for 25 minutes to cook the veg and let all the various flavours blend.

When the vegetables in the soup are tender, pour in the tins of beans.

I have to admit that I go overboard here and often add a third tin. Rinse the beans by emptying the tins into a sieve or colander and running them under cold water for a while.

Stir the beans into the soup. You may need to add some more water at this point; this soup has a thin stock with plenty of veg, bacon and beans floating around in it.

Once the soup is hot and everything is cooked, break the pasta into 3cm/1in pieces and stir in. The heat of the soup will usually cook the pasta if you leave the pan lid on tight.

Check seasoning.

Serve with a sprinkling of grated strong cheddar cheese on top.

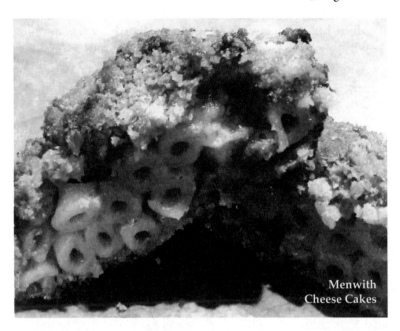

Menwith
Cheese Cakes

MENWITH CHEESE CAKES

I always associate macaroni cheese with America – and the place in the north where Americans spring to mind is Menwith Hill.

Originally an RAF base between Otley, Pateley Bridge and Harrogate, and perched on the Nidderdale moors, its large 'golf ball' structures draw curious eyes.

Leased to the US Air Force, it was constructed in 1954 as a 'communication intercept and intelligence support service', becoming one of their most powerful 'listening' centres during the Cold War. Menwith Hill remains in secret use today, but I'm sure they would love this novel recipe for left -over mac 'n' cheese.

Macaroni and cheese is not the easiest thing to make right. It must be very creamy and quite soft. I tend not to bake it in the oven for too long as it swells up the pasta and dries the sauce.

Made hot with a quick grill to brown the top is best.

And it is this soft and creamy texture that, when cold, makes the best cakes.

Ingredients
macaroni and cheese;
1pint of whole milk;
¼ pint of double cream (optional);
30g flour;
30g butter;
200g strong cheese (grated) or blue cheese for a more adult version;
250g dried macaroni pasta;
1 teaspoon French mustard (optional but worth it);
salt and fresh ground black pepper;
handful crushed cornflakes

Method
Make a roux sauce, melt the butter in a pan, add flour and cook for a minute... it should look like a soft ball.

Gradually add milk and whisk after each addition. Use enough milk to make a thick sauce about the texture of un-whipped double cream. Let the sauce bubble for a minute, whisking frequently so that it does not burn on the pan bottom.

Add the grated cheese and mustard and whisk into the sauce. If the sauce is too thick, pour in some of the double cream or use water to let the sauce down a touch. Season with pepper but be careful with the salt, as there is usually enough of it in the cheese already.

Meanwhile, bring a large pan of salted water to the boil. Once done, add the pasta and continue to boil until it is just cooked.

Drain the pasta and add it to the sauce. Season with plenty of pepper and a bit more mustard if you wish.

If the mixture is too stiff, then add some more cream or water. Ideally, it needs to be quite runny.

Pour into a dish and sprinkle on some more cheese mixed with a handful of crushed cornflakes – and then grill until it is bubbling and golden.

MAC AND CHEESE CAKES

Ingredients
left-over mac and cheese;
1 or 2 beaten eggs
(depending on how much
mac and cheese being used);
50g flour (seasoned with
pepper and salt and a touch
of mixed herbs);
150g breadcrumbs or
crushed cornflakes;
oil for frying (deep or
shallow, it's up to you. What
do you feel safest with?)

Method
Best to prepare your
'station' first for coating;
having everything ready in
dishes saves time and
frustration.

Put your seasoned flour
onto a large plate. Have the
beaten eggs in a dish and
the crushed flakes or bread
crumbs on another large
plate; finally you need a
plate for your end product.

Take a tablespoon of the
cold mac and cheese and
form a burger shape in the
palm of your hand. Cover in
flour then dip in the egg and
finally coat in the cornflakes
or breadcrumbs. If nothing
sticks, repeat the process.

Keep going until all the
mac and cheese is used up
and you have a plate of
coated cakes.

Chill until needed.

Once you are ready to
serve, take the cakes out and
allow them to return to
room temperature.

Deep fry for about three
minutes until golden and
heated through, otherwise
put a good layer of oil in the
bottom of a heavy pan and
fry on a medium heat for
about three minutes each
side, or until they are golden
brown and heated through.

Whichever way I am
frying them, I always offer
one cake up to break open
and test to see if it is hot all
the way through.

Fabulous as a supper or a
starter. Great too as a buffet
snack with a spicy dip.

Mrs Whymes'
Singing Hinnies

MRS WHYMES' SINGING HINNIES

This recipe was given to me by a good friend of our family. His mother, Mrs Whymes, used to make them up in Shields in Northumberland.

The title of these beauties originates from the north east, Hinny being a term of endearment coming from the word honey. 'Singing' comes from the sound of the cakes sizzling in the butter.

Ingredients
250g self-raising flour;
pinch of salt;
25g sugar;
50g butter (very cold);
50g lard (very cold);
100g currants;
zest of 1 lemon;
1 egg with 2 tablespoons of milk

Method
Sift the flour into a baking bowl, cut the cold fats into small pieces and rub into the flour using your fingertips.

Rub in as quickly as you can so that the fat stays relatively cold – this gives you a lighter result. Once the mixture resembles fine breadcrumbs add currants, sugar and lemon zest.

Beat the egg with the milk and add to the flour mixture a little at a time (depending on the size of the egg you may not need it all). Bring the dough together to form a soft but pliable texture.

Lightly flour the surface and roll out the dough until it's about the thickness of a pound coin. Pre-heat a large heavy frying pan or griddle. Using a piece of buttered paper lightly rub the hot griddle/pan.

Add the cut hinnies and gently cook for 3-5 minutes each side. If you roll the hinnies out too thickly, they will brown before they are cooked in the centre.

Serve fresh, spread with butter, but they will keep for about a day. Gently warm on a griddle to re-serve.

13

Out of the Box Scones

OUT OF THE BOX SCONE

Outside the Box is a fabulous organisation based in Ilkley, West Yorkshire.

They support people with complex needs to work in their own café.

These young people access all aspects... learning to serve the public, be a barista brewing fresh coffee and preparing and serving delicious lunches.

In return the public are welcomed, and served a delightful well-presented and cost-effective meal.

Those working there need to be able to make and master relatively simple and understandable items that are also appetising and delicious.

These scones fill that remit; any amount can be made if you keep the cup the same size.

Decide which cup/beaker/pot you want to use.

Pre-heated oven: Gas 6, 400f, 200c, 180 fan

Ingredients
for 12 medium scones
4 cups self-raising flour (I have used a standard teacup);
1 teaspoon baking powder (1 tsp for every 4 cups);
1 cup of lemonade (not diet);
1 cup of double cream

Method
Simply mix all of the above together until just combined. As with all scones, do not over mix as this can make the mixture tough. Tip the dough onto a lightly floured surface and pat the mixture out until a good 2cm or ¼ in thick.

Using a cutter, cut the scone out using a sharp direct press. Do not twist the cutter through the dough as this can often bind the sides of the scone together and they will not raise straight.

Place on a baking tray, lightly greased or lined with baking paper, leaving a good gap between the scones. Brush the top with a little milk (or what is left of the double cream) and bake for up to 15 minutes or until golden.

Serve with jam and lashings of butter.

For variations, you can add fruit, cherries and some almond extract or, if feeling adventurous, some chopped ginger or 1 tsp of ground ginger, while replacing the lemonade with ginger beer.

Scones will freeze, but do not store well. However, these are so easy to rustle up you can make as needed.

Out of the Box Scones – Savoury

SUNDRIED TOMATO AND FETA SCONES

There are many different types and flavours of bread flour available. For these scones, I have used sundried tomato and garlic flour.

You can continue to use the lemonade, as it is not over sweet.

Ingredients
4 cups of flour;
2 teaspoons of baking powder;
200g feta crumbled;
1 cup lemonade;
1 cup double cream

Method
Measure out the flour and baking powder, crumble in the feta cheese and mix in the lemonade and cream.

Lightly knead the mixture on a floured board, pat out to 2cm in thickness and cut out.

It may be an idea to cut these savoury scones into squares. Either way, serve with butter and chutney.

ROMAN CHICKEN

In a Roman cookery book called *Apicius*, it is first suggested that a mixture of herbs, spelt and bread were used to stuff 'chicken, dormouse, hare and pig.'

Thousands of years later we are still using stuffing of various types.

In around 7AD, 5,000 Romans from the Ninth Legion, under the orders of Governor Quintus Petillius Cerialis, marched from Lincoln north to tackle the upstart Brigantes, ancient Britons, who held much of the eastern side of the region.

They settled in a place where the River Foss joins the River Ouse, which and could transport men and supplies in from the North Sea. York was also an excellent settlement to monitor the northern tribes and those from the west. It is entirely possible that, after battling and fighting, the Romans sat down to chicken and stuffing.

This dish is ideal to make in advance and great served with mayonnaise or a Greek yogurt dip.

The same method will apply to fingers of salmon or indeed slices of belly pork (although that will require longer slower cooking).

Pre-heated oven: Gas 5, 375f, 190c, 170 fan

Ingredients
1 chicken fillet per person; 1 egg for every 2 fillets; 200g of your favourite stuffing mix per 2 fillets (I like to use the more adventurous flavours e.g. apple and thyme, or whole meal, cider apple and rosemary etc.); 2-3 tablespoons of oil

Method
Cut the chicken breast into long fingers. Some will be longer than others as you reach the edge of the fillet, this is not an issue.

You could make them all nugget size if you wish, but you will have to alter the cooking time as overcooked will result in very dry meat.

Beat the egg and place on a plate or large flat dish.

Take the dry stuffing mix and tip it into the bowl of a food processor or blender. Blitz the stuffing to a finer grade otherwise you have a very chunky over-crunchy coating that overpowers the tender chicken, but don't overdo it or you will have dust and that will not be too appetising.

Place the stuffing coating on a large dinner plate or flat dish and a clean baking tray or plate to lay your prepared chicken on.

Roman Chicken

Keeping one hand clean (in case the phone rings or you need to answer the door) dip each chicken strip into the egg, then gently drop it into the stuffing and coat, sprinkling and flicking the stuffing over the top of the chicken strip, a bit like bathing a baby!

Lay the coated strip onto the clean tray. Repeat the method until all the chicken has been used up. If you have some stuffing and egg left over, mix the two together, adding a little hot water if needed, roll into balls and bake along with the chicken strips.

The chicken can be kept in the fridge until you are ready to cook. It is worth noting, if you want to cook them straight away, that it is best to try give them at least 30 minutes in the fridge to firm up.

If the chicken was fresh and hasn't yet been frozen, you can open-freeze the uncooked chicken on a tray. Once frozen store in a freezer tub and take out when required.

Using a large flat lipped oven tray, or roasting tin, heat the oil in the pre-heated oven, lay the chicken in one layer on the tray and return to the oven, turning halfway through cooking.

The chicken strips will take about 20-25 minutes, depending on thickness.

Alternatively, fry on the top of the stove in a hot pan with a little oil. Frying the strips this way is delicious, but there is a chance that the chicken may break up and some of the coating break off, although those crunchy bits can be served alongside.

Yogurt dip
Greek yogurt (strained type); plenty ground black pepper; pinch of salt
Options: chopped fresh herbs (including mint, coriander, parsley and chives); finely chopped fresh chilli; good spoonful of pesto; lemon zest and more black pepper.

Swaledale Lamb
and Mint Pies

Swaledale Pies –
Second helping!

SWALEDALE LAMB AND MINT PIES

When driving or walking in the countryside, there is something reassuring about seeing sheep contentedly grazing in fields of green.

Swaledale are one such breed that thrives in and around our rugged terrain.

They are a hardy animal suited for exposed regions, make excellent mums and will rear lambs in adverse conditions.

Their wool supports a profitable cottage industry of knitting – producing warm cosy quality jumpers – and their meat is succulent, lean and sought after. To coin a well-known phrase in these parts, 'waste not, want not.'

I always make these pies in tart tins very much like a mince pie. They are great to freeze, handy for lunches, a quick tea, or to take with you on a picnic.

Make sure you label the pies if you freeze them. Don't be like me and end up with a UFO (unidentified frozen object). Mum often rang me to ask if she needed gravy or custard for the pie she had just rescued from a frozen recess.

As with the majority of pastry recipes in this book, the method and amounts are the same, but there are times when I vary the flour.

Please don't be shy and hold back on which flour to use. There are many unusual tasty flours on the market.

For these pies I have used wholemeal flour, but how about some dried mint in the pastry?

Make the pastry in the same way as the recipe in part 5 of this book.

Using 500g of flour will make quite a lot of mini pies which can then be frozen.

Filling
1lb of minced lamb;
1 large onion;
1 lamb stock cube;
glug of red wine (plus a glass for yourself);
1 medium diced potato;
1 small leek finely diced;

23

1-2 tablespoon of mint sauce from a jar;
1 tablespoon flour;
1–3 cloves of garlic crushed;
little oil for frying;
1 egg
Pre-heated oven: Gas 4, 350f, 180c, 160 fan

Method

Use a casserole dish that can go on the stove and in the oven, so you retain all the flavours by not transferring.

Finely dice the onion, garlic and leek and fry in the oil. Remove when soft.

Using the same pan, fry the mince. Depending on how fatty it is, you may need to spoon off some of the fat, but mince is such high quality now there is often very little residue.

Return the onions, leeks etc and sprinkle over the spoon of flour. It will all look a bit messy, but once the flour has cooked for a minute you can start to add the wine, stock cube and some water – approximately 300mls depending on how thick you want your gravy. Season well with salt and pepper (remember to taste it) then add the mint sauce.

Place the casserole in a slow oven about 120c Gas 2. Leave to braise for up to two hours and keep checking and stirring, adding a little more water (or wine) if the mixture becomes too thick.

While the meat is cooking, roll out the chilled pastry and cut circles just a little larger than the tart tin.

Once the meat has cooked and cooled, line each tart tin with a disc of pastry and pack with a good dessertspoon of filling.

Brush the lid or second circle with egg and lay over the filling and bottom circle. Crimp the edges together, making sure they stick.

Make a small knife incision in the top of each pie, brush with egg and bake for 35-40 minutes.

Cool in the tin slightly before removing carefully and allowing to cool completely.

THE DALES CRACKER

Cheese-making first came to the Yorkshire Dales during the 12th Century, when Cistercian monks brought the art to the monasteries at Fors, Jervaulx and Fountains.

The cheese was in the main from sheeps' milk.

However, following the dissolution of the monasteries, the art of cheese-making became farm based and there was a transition to cows, which were more plentiful for the farmers.

These biscuits are very easy to make, but they won't be ready to eat for a couple of days. I must say I was quite impressed when I came up with this little gem.

They look and taste fabulous, with that real artisan feel about them.

I have made them for gifts, presented on a board (made by my beautiful nephew, Caleb) with a small truckle of cheese from the Wensleydale Creamery at Hawes in the heavenly Yorkshire Dales.

Pre-heated oven: Gas 4, 350f, 180c, 160 fan
Grease and line a 1lb loaf tin.

Ingredients
3 egg whites;
100g caster sugar;
200g plain flour white or wholemeal;
300g combination of the following:
pistachio nuts, walnut, almonds, hazel nuts, cranberries, sultanas, pumpkin seeds, sunflower seeds, oats;pinch of dried chilli, 2 teaspoons mixed herbs; parsley; 1tsp freshly course ground black pepper; flaked sea salt.

These are but a few of the fillings. Try anything you like that goes with cheese.

The Dales Cracker

Method

Firstly, prepare all the fillings.

Combine the nuts, seeds and spices to whatever combination you fancy.

I would say it's not ideal to mix them all. Try and keep to two larger items and two additional flavourings, for example, pistachio sultana and chilli.

It is always worth adding some salt and pepper to support the other flavours. When combined set aside.

In a clean, dry bowl, whisk the egg whites until foamy and start to add in the sugar little by little until you have smooth stiff stable meringue.

Fold in the flour and, filling gently, mix until all well combined (do not over mix).

Place this mixture into the greased loaf tin and slightly level the top.

Bake in the pre-heated oven until firm to the touch and it just starts to change colour on top.

Leave in the tin to cool for a few minutes and then lift onto the wire rack to cool completely.

When cold, wrap the loaf in greaseproof paper and foil and leave to one side for at least one day, ideally two.

Pre-heat oven to 120c gas 1 or 2. Using a very sharp serrated knife slice the loaf into very thin slices, about ½ cm or thinner if you can.

Lay the slices in one layer on baking trays, there could be about 30 to 40, place in the oven and leave for a good 30-40 minutes or until they become crisp but not coloured.

They may not be crisp in the oven, but once cold they will certainly become so.

Store in an air-tight tin.

THE GROWLER

Yorkshire slang for a raised pie, 'The Growler' is most probably adapted from the NAAFI Army and Navy word for similar.

A growler was a pail used to carry beer home from the pub. The escaping gas would rumble around the galvanised bucket making a 'growling' sound. Maybe the raised hot water pastry resembled a bucket which carried the meat.

We are famous for our pork pies here in the north and I have been privileged to taste quite a few.

Quite honestly, I didn't get a body like mine from not eating them!

This recipe may be seen as a bit of a cheat, but it is rather foolproof – and food-wise. Nothing says Merry Christmas better than a pie.

I have used meat that I cooked separately, which does two things. It allows you to choose combinations you want and controls the amount of 'juice' that can burst through the wall of your pie.

If you prefer to use 'jelly' and have a traditional style pie, that will work equally as well. But, in this recipe, I have used stuffing between the meat layers.

If you choose not to use the layer of stuffing, use another couple of layers of meat and then add the jelly.

You do not have to use the same meats I have given you here, but make sure you use meat with plenty of flavour.

Grease a 2lb loaf tin or 8in round cake tin.
Pre-heated oven: Gas 4, 350f, 180c, 160 fan

Pastry ingredients
450g plain flour;
1 teaspoon freshly ground black pepper;
1 teaspoon salt;
125ml water;
150g lard (cut into cubes);
1 egg (beaten) for glazing

The Growler

Method

Place the flour, salt and pepper in a baking bowl.

Put the water and lard into a small pan and melt over a low heat.

Making a well in the centre of the flour, pour in the melted lard and water, mixing carefully as the pastry will be hot.

Once the pastry has come together to form a soft ball, wrap in cling film for five minutes.

Divide the pastry into roughly two-thirds and third. Roll out the two-thirds piece between two pieces of cling film.

Use this to line the tin, making sure you leave an overhang.

Fill the pie with the pre-cooked meat (see below

instructions) dab the edge of the pie with beaten egg.

Roll out the third piece again between two pieces of cling film and lay over the pie. Trim and crimp the edges. Decorate the top with cut-out pieces of pastry and give the whole pie a good brush with the beaten egg. Finally, before you put the pie in the oven make a hole in the top to let out some steam while it is baking.

Pie filling
It's a good idea to have this ready and cooked before you start the pastry. It can even be prepared the day before. Use whatever meat you like. It can also be made with game.

Stuffing:
If you choose to use the stuffing layer you can either use fresh homemade stuffing or use a good quality bought one – there are some great flavours on the market and some real artisan and local specialists

making packet stuffing. I've used an apple and cider stuffing with rosemary.

Filling ingredients
2 chicken breasts;
1 large slice of smoked gammon;
1 packet of stuffing mix;
4 pork tenderloin steaks;
1 onion finely chopped;
salt and freshly ground black pepper

Method
Lay the chicken breast on a board and cover with a piece of cling film, using a meat hammer or rolling pin and bash the chicken firmly but carefully until very thin, about ½ cm in thickness.

Repeat this with the pork steak and smoked gammon. Fry the flattened meat in batches until brown. Once cooked, put the meat on a plate and set aside.

Make up the stuffing as per the instruction on the packet. Add in the finely chopped onion. Lay the cooked meat in alternate layers with the stuffing between, repeat until all the meat and stuffing has been used and the pie is full.

Don't forget to pour on any meat juice left on the plate.

Bake the pie in a pre-heated oven for about an hour or until it is a rich golden dark brown. (Remember the content of the pie is cooked, so no worries about it being raw).

Leave the pie in the tin to cool for a good 30 minutes and gently turn out and allow to cool completely.

If you have decided not to use the stuffing, then you would now fill the pie with the jelly.

Jelly:
1 very good quality stock (jelly) cube;
3 leaves of gelatine.
Soak the gelatine leaves in cold water for 10 minutes.

Pour half a pint of boiling water over the stock cube and allow to dissolve.

Squeeze the gelatine of excess cold water and add to the hot stock.

Using a small funnel inserted into the hole in the top of the pie, gently pour and fill.

Leave the pie to set which could take up to two hours.

Best served cold with some pickle or a fabulous tangy pickled onion.

'F'T PROPER DINNER OR TEA'

A term used to describe the main meal of the day,
either served at lunch time (dinner time) or evening (tea time).

CATTERICK HASH

GREEK STREET PIE

HOLMFIRTH SMILING BEEF

MACCLESFIELD POSH POBS

NONE GO BYE MEATBALLS

PRESTON CATHOLIC PIE

SHEPHERDS PURSE LENTIL SLICE

SHIPLEY SPUDS

SUMMAT QUICK F'TEA

WHITBY CHOWDER

Catterick Hash

CATTERICK HASH

The story of corned beef is of a British name given to an Irish dish, 'corn' relating to the size of the salt crystals used to cure the meat.

The corned beef we commonly use today was very much a staple diet of our troops, from the Boer war to the Second World War, where it formed a large part of the rations served with a hardtack biscuit.

The popularity of corned beef became such that wherever British Troops were stationed in the world, the local community adopted it for themselves.

Here in the north of England, we have an army base at Catterick coupled with one of the recovery units for Help for Heroes, and this recipe is a salute to you guys.

Since my *Bake Off* days, I have been privileged to work with some of their recovering veterans, their cooking and baking tirelessly supporting some of the under-privileged young people I run a cooking club for.

These two worlds of injured veterans and hard-to-reach kids would never otherwise have come together, so it warms my heart to think that I'm a part of that.

We all have a version of corned beef hash and this one is healthy, tasty, chunky and useful, which means it's great for a pie filling or with a savoury crumble on top.

Ingredients
500g large potatoes;
1 large onion;
300g carrots;
1 beef stock cube (jellied type);
1 large tin of corned beef (chilled);
1 leek;
200g turnip;
salt and pepper;
150g frozen peas

Method

As a rule, I always keep my tin of corned beef in the fridge, it helps when slicing it up.

Peel the potatoes, carrots and turnip, cut into chunks and boil in salted water until tender. Slice the leeks and onions and sauté until soft and golden brown.

Drain the potatoes, turnip and carrots and break with a fork until the veg is well mixed together.

While the mixture is hot, stir in the stock pot, but be careful not to break down the veg too much or you will end up with mush.

Mix into the veg and stock the fried onions and leeks, season to taste. Do not at this stage use too much salt as the corned beef is usually salty enough.

Open the corned beef and cut into 2cm cubes. This may sound like quite large chunks, but the corned beef does break during mixing.

Add the peas and mix carefully, checking on the seasoning all the way.

You can now heat it through on the stove top but continue to be gentle with your stirring.

I prefer to put in it in the oven to heat through, so that everything stays chunky.

GREEK STREET PIE

This pie's ingredients are predominantly Greek – filo pastry and ricotta cheese – so what better than to name it after a street in Leeds city centre?

One can only assume that the name was given over to where Greek merchants or immigrants came together to form a community.

Greek Street is now a bustling centre for offices. It sits on the edge of the area where many legal firms are situated and hosts many bars and restaurants.

This pie is fabulous at any time of year. It is sometimes called Easter Pie as it contains hard boiled eggs, a symbol of that time.

It is great as a buffet dish, but equally delicious for a family meal served with a chopped salad, something a bit different for vegetarians.

If you've never used filo pastry before don't worry its very forgiving in this pie and patching up is allowed.

There are a few stages with this recipe, but work methodically and remember that it can be all kept in the fridge even overnight before you want to assemble and bake the pie.

Pre-heated oven: Gas 6, 400f, 200c, 180 fan

Ingredients

1 packet of filo pastry (plus 2 tablespoons of oil or melted butter for brushing the pastry);
300g ricotta cheese;
1 bag of fresh spinach or 6 balls from a bag of frozen;
50g of pine nuts (toasted if desired);
1 large onion finely chopped;
1 clove of garlic (crushed);
freshly grated nutmeg;
freshly ground black pepper;
100g parmesan shavings;
1 whole egg beaten;
4-6 hard-boiled eggs (depending on persons);
salt
7in flan case

Greek Street Pie

38

Method

First put the eggs on to boil, everyone has their own method.

I bring the water to a boil, put in the eggs, let the water come back to the boil for about one minute, remove the pan from the heat and let the eggs sit in the hot water for about 10 minutes.

Put the eggs into cold water to stop the cooking, then peel when cold.

Chop and fry the onions and garlic in a little oil until golden, grate in the nutmeg and the salt and pepper depending on your taste.

Set this aside.

Prepare the spinach.

If using frozen, defrost and drain well.

If fresh, put in a pan with two tablespoons of hot water. Put the lid on, let the water come to boil, remove the pan from the heat, leave the lid on and in about five minutes the spinach will have wilted, ready to use.

Mix the spinach and onions, along with the beaten egg, into the ricotta cheese, taste and season well. Stir in the pine nuts and parmesan cheese.

Line a pie dish with filo pastry brushing each layer lightly with oil. Lay the edges over the side of the dish. Use about five sheets.

Fill the pastry with the cheese mixture and smooth over the top.

Cut the hard-boiled eggs in half lengthways and lay them face down around the dish (like a clock face)

Lay more layers of filo on top of the pie and use the last three to four sheets of filo in a more scrunched up manner to create a rough covering.

Make sure the top is brushed with oil.

Sprinkle on a few salt flakes (optional) and bake for about 25 minutes or until the top is a deep golden brown.

This pie is best served warm or just aired.

Holmfirth
Smiling Beef

HOLMFIRTH SMILING BEEF

Why, you might ask, is this dish called Smiling Beef?

All I can say is that if you spend the best part of a cooking day accompanied by a bottle of red wine, you'll be smiling.

Holmfirth has a very successful vineyard, so the cooking and drinking go together especially well for this dish.

The privately-owned winery grows both red and white grapes which have been especially cultivated for cooler climates.

All the vines are planted by hand and ready for harvesting around the end of October. The good news is you can visit the vineyard and have a wine tasting.

I also advocate that you should never cook with what you're not prepared to drink.

In other words, there is no such thing as 'cooking wine'. Good food deserves similar wine.

Beef cheeks are currently inexpensive, so very tasty and not too popular, so have a go at this before they become fashionable.

This is an impressive dish but so easy to make.

All that is needed is a pile of creamy mash, sautéed leeks and some green veg.

And why not go the whole hog and whisk up a Yorkshire?

I love my slow cooker and use it for many things. However, I reckon this is one recipe that needs that 'baked' taste from long oven cooking.

Some modern ovens have a slow oven installed. That is excellent, otherwise use the lowest setting.

Pre-heated oven: Gas 1, 275f, 140c, 120 fan (if your oven can go lower, please use that)

Part 2

Ingredients
Depending on the size,
1 beef cheek per person;
1 large onion finely chopped;
3 cloves of garlic (crushed);
1 very good beef stock cube
(I use the jelly type);
2 tablespoons oil;

1 bottle of decent red wine
(only cook with what you'd
be prepared to drink);
2 tablespoons flour and 25g
soft butter mashed together
to create a paste (for
thickening the gravy later)

Method
Using a pot that can go in
the oven as well as on top,
add the onions to the hot oil.

When brown and golden
add the garlic (be careful not
to burn the garlic) to the
stock pot and mix into the
onions.

Add the beef and let it
brown for five minutes each
side. Pour on the wine until
it comes halfway up the
pieces of beef, season with
salt and pepper.

Put the lid on the pot and
place in the oven. Leave this
to cook as long as possible.
Put it in the oven before you
go to bed and turn it out
when you get up – a good
eight hours is ideal.

Afterwards, take the pot
and place it on the stove top.
Carefully lift out the meat.

The cheeks will give way,
so use a large spoon to put
them on a plate for a few
minutes.

Bring the liquid to the
boil and teaspoon by
teaspoon whisk in the flour
and butter paste.

You may not require it all,
it depends on how thick you
want the gravy.

Allow this to bubble for a
few minutes to cook the
flour before lifting the
cheeks back in and tucking
them tenderly under their
blanket of boozy gravy.

MACCLESFIELD POSH POBS

Pobs is bread soaked in hot milk and sugar, eaten by the poor but also given to the sick who were recuperating.

In Macclesfield in 1886, a new style of bread was being manufactured which contained wheat germ this loaf and had the brand name baked into the side, so Hovis was born.

It was named after a national competition won by Herbert Grime, the name coming from the latin term *hominis vis* (strength of man).

This tart is somewhat quiche-like. It's great to make ahead and bake just before you need it.

It can be left in the fridge the night before and is a bit like a savoury bread and butter pudding.

Pre-heated oven: Gas 6, 400f, 200c, 180 fan

Grease an 8in cake tin or tart ring.

Ingredients
200g stale white bread cut into 2cm cubes;
6 free range eggs;
250ml double cream;
200g smoked bacon (chopped and fried);
1 large onion finely chopped;
150g strong cheddar cheese grated;
Salt and freshly ground black pepper;
2 teaspoons mixed herbs (either fresh or dried)

Method
Fry the bacon and chopped onion, set aside when cooked and crisp.

Whisk the eggs with the seasoning and double cream.

Put the cubed bread in the greased tin and arrange so that there is an even layer over the bottom.

Sprinkle on the bacon and onion, grated cheese and mixed herbs.

Macclesfield
Posh Pobs

Pour over the egg and cream mixture and gently press the bread down into the egg until it is saturated with the egg mixture.

Cover the whole thing with cling film or place a plate on top and put in the fridge, preferably leaving overnight.

Pre-heat the oven before you place the tart tin on a baking sheet and bake until the bread is golden and crisp to the touch.

Let the tart stand for five minutes before serving with a lovely green salad.

Alternatives: In place of the bacon use lardons or, before baking, use chopped smoked salmon.

Why not beat some herbed cream cheese into the egg and cream mixture?

You could use chopped, fried mushrooms and a blue cheese, there is opportunity for experimentation!

None Go Bye
Meatballs

NONE GO BYE MEATBALLS

Along an old Yorkshire Turnpike Road stands the farm of 'None Go Bye', and there are two stories as to why it is so called.

A resting and watering establishment for coach travellers, after the sharp steep pull up from Otley or long haul from Harrogate, both horses and men would need rest and refreshments and here was the place that none would go by.

Alternatively, imagine a moonlit night and the stage-coach hurtling along the turnpike road. Hiding in the shadows was the notorious Dick Turpin, majestic on his trusty steed Black Bess. He steps out: "None go by".

When I go to 'None Go Bye's farm shop, I'm never hijacked but I do get the best mince and sausage.

Other fabulous fresh meat and bread, flour and potatoes are on sale all served with a smile.

Plus, I can visit the animals, go fishing or just sit and watch the day go by.

These meatballs are so easy to make and every time I serve them they have that wow factor, served steaming hot with a little sprinkling of parsley over top.

The secret is not to roll them too tight, just about the size of a golf ball and just squeezed enough to hold the shape.

Ingredients

500gms minced beef;
500gms sausages (vary the taste by using sausages of your choice, e.g., pork and leek, chorizo style);
1 large onion;
3 cloves of garlic;

1 large tin chopped tomato;
1 small carton of pasata;
half a tube tomato puree;
1 teaspoon mixed herbs;
1 teaspoon of chopped chilli;
3 tablespoons oil;
salt and pepper

Method

Split the sausage and put the filling in a bowl, add the mince and mix both together well.

Roll into as many balls as you can but don't make them too small as they can become tough and hard.

Add the oil to the frying pan and heat, add the meatballs and cook until brown.

They don't have to be cooked all the way through as they will continue to cook in the sauce.

For the Sauce: Chop the onion and the garlic, put 1tbs oil in a pan and fry.

Add the chopped tomato, pasata and the puree along with the chilli. Add the mixed herbs and season with salt and pepper, allow to simmer and thicken.

When the sauce is ready put in the browned meatballs, bake in the oven for about 30 minutes to allow the meatballs to cook and properly heat through.

PRESTON CATHOLIC PIE

During the Reformation, Lancashire maintained quite a lot of its Catholic inhabitants, accounting during the 17th and 18th centuries for nearly a fifth of the population.

During the Irish famine many left and settled directly across from their homeland where they were welcomed with work in the mill towns.

One such area was Preston, and their new Irish residents were loyal to the tradition that Catholics did not eat meat on Fridays.

Thus, with their love of potatoes and the replacement of butter for meat, the Preston butter pie was born. Very much a northern dish, it is full of love, taste and carbs!

This is fabulous served

with some peppery greens or a tin of baked beans.

I have made the bold choice to use different flour for this pastry having come across onion flour, (normal white bread flour but with added onion.)

This pie can be made the traditional way or use brown flour.

Pre-heated oven: Gas 4, 350f, 180c, 160 fan
8in Pie plate

Ingredients
200g onion infused bread;
flour / plain flour;
50g butter;
50g white fat (lard, dripping or Trex);
pinch of salt;
cold water (to bind pastry);
1 egg (beaten)

Filling
3 large potatoes (not new);
1 large onion;
100g butter;
50g butter (to slice between the layers)

Method
First make the pastry, put the flour and salt in a baking bowl, dice the butter and white fat into the flour.

Rub using fingertips until the mixture resembles fine breadcrumbs.

Using a knife to mix add two tablespoons of water mix with the knife until the dough comes together.

Pull the pastry together using your hands, don't be tempted to add more water.

When the dough is firmly pressed together in a ball flatten slightly, wrap in greaseproof paper and chill for a least 30 minutes.

(The pastry can be made in advance and frozen)

While the pastry is chilling, peel potatoes and cut into thick slices, part boil until just soft.

Peel and slice the onion, sauté in the 100g of butter over a low heat until soft.

Drain the potatoes and put to one side.

Roll out two-thirds of the pastry and line a pie plate.

49

Preston Catholic Pie

Layer with potatoes and onions then knobs of butter from the 50g. Repeat until all the filling is used up.

Roll out the top with the remaining pastry.

Brush the edge of the pie with beaten egg, lay over the top, press the edges together, trim and crimp the edge of the pie.

Make a couple of holes in the top and brush the lid of the pie with beaten egg.

Bake in the pre-heated oven for about 30–45 minutes until the pie is golden brown.

Shepherds Purse
Lentil Sauce

52

SHEPHERDS PURSE LENTIL SAUCE

A fabulous lady called Judy Bell began making cheese from her own sheep in 1989.

She went on to produce cheeses from cows and buffalo milk which resulted in an awarding-winning blue variety.

Harrogate Blue has a mellow, nutty flavour, creamy and satisfying. It won gold at the World Cheese Awards in 2019 and super gold in 2017, ranking the 11th best in the world.

Yorkshire Blue is similarly mild and a perfect introduction to the world of blue cheese, once again winning many awards.

It took gold in the 2019 World Cheese Awards and has ranked highly at the prestigious Nantwich International Cheese Show.

Nowadays, Shepherds Purse is run by Katie and Caroline, Judy's daughters.

The name is taken from a plant with a flower that looks something like the purse a shepherd would use when out tending the flock.

Versatile, this can be vegetarian, a main course or starter, a fabulous buffet table dish and perfect for a picnic. Made deep dish or shallow, eaten hot or cold, the result is incredibly tasty.

Add other ingredients to make the dish your own, such as diced peppers, cooked mushrooms or a scattering of chilli flakes. *Pre-heated oven: Gas 5, 375f, 109c,170 fan*

Ingredients
240g red lentils (washed);
480ml water;
1 vegetable or chicken stock cube (the jelly type);
1 large onion finely chopped;
1 tablespoon oil;
1 clove of crushed garlic;
3 eggs;
150–200g Shepherd's Purse blue cheese (Harrogate Blue or Yorkshire Blue);
freshly milled black pepper and salt to taste.

Part 2

Method

Place the water, lentils and stock in a large pan and bring to the boil. Turn the heat down and simmer, stirring occasionally until all the water has been taken up by the lentils and they are very soft. A little more water may need to be added.

While the lentils are cooking, fry the chopped onion and garlic in a little oil until soft and translucent.

If you are using peppers and/or mushrooms cook them along with the onion and garlic.

Give the lentils a good mix and make sure they resemble a smooth mash type consistency. Add in the onions etc. Taste.

Now add salt and pepper but keep tasting. Most pulses take quite a bit of salt, but are not very nice when over-salted. Add at this point any herbs or spices.

While the mixture is still warm, crumble in the cheese and mix well. Meanwhile, beat the eggs and stir into the lentil and cheese mixture.

Pour the mixture into a greased tin or baking dish. A Swiss roll tin is good if you want to make a shallow handy buffet dish, or a greased cake tin if you want to make a main course, which will cut into thick wedges.

Bake in a pre-heated oven for about 40 minutes or until the top is beginning to brown and bubble.

Do not over bake as the slice will become dry, especially if you are making the thinner version.

Serve at room temperature with a fresh chopped salad. It is also fabulous served as a paté-style dish with French bread or crackers.

You can try this with other cheeses, but make sure you use a good tasty one. Quality over quantity is key.

SHIPLEY SPUDS

After the Second World War young people from all over Italy came to work in West Yorkshire's textile industry.

Many of them were girls employed in factories in and around Bradford.

To give the newcomers a home, a hostel was built on Otley Road, Shipley, which housed eight and then 24 and then finally 40 of them.

Apparently, they had a lot of fun chatting and cooking with each other, despite the kitchens being cramped and rations sparse.

One can only imagine that in this corner of England garlic and other herbs were not easy to find or even heard of back then.

Many of the Italian girls attended English lessons at Belle Vue Upper School. They loved their new life in Yorkshire, not forgetting to send money home to their parents in Italy. Some would go on to marry, often in the Catholic church of St Aidan by an Italian priest from the Italian Mission in Bradford.

This recipe picks up on their influence.

A classy little side dish, it can be made vegetarian by omitting the smoked bacon and is fabulous if you want to make things ahead of time such as a dinner party.

I like to leave the skins on the potatoes if they are nice and clean with not too many 'eyes'.

Serves 4
Pre-heated oven: Gas 5, 375f,
190c,170 fan

Ingredients
1 medium/large baking potato per person;
3-4 large plump cloves of garlic (or a couple more to taste if you wish);
200g chopped smoked bacon (optional);
2 teaspoons salt;
2 teaspoons freshly ground black pepper;
400g mascarpone cheese

Shipley Spuds

Method

If you want to peel the potatoes do so and then dice.

Place the potatoes into plenty of boiling salted water, lower the heat to a simmer and boil for 10 minutes.

(This will all depend on the softness of your potato, keep checking after five).

When a knife pushed into the potato offers a little resistance, that is time to drain them.

While the potatoes are simmering, fry the bacon until crisp.

Use a large frying pan – big enough to take all the potatoes.

When the bacon is cooked and crisp, toss in the warm potatoes together with the crushed garlic, mascarpone, salt and pepper. Mix thoroughly.

The potatoes may break up a bit, but this only adds to the deliciousness of the finished dish.

Pile the mixture into a heat-proof dish and bake for about 40 minutes until bubbling and golden brown on top.

SUMMAT QUICK F'TEA

I love listening to dialects.

There are so many prominent ones across the north of England – even between the borders of West and South Yorkshire.

It can be like stepping into a different country when you hear the locals talk.

My grandad Driver was a true Dalesman and worked in farming and with horses for much of his young life, until he had to take up employment in the wool mills of Aireborough.

Alex Driver – or 'Elek' as he used to pronounce his name – could say things that

very few would understand.
And he would often need
something rustled up
quickly for his tea.

This is a quick, tasty
recipe that can use up
leftovers, although you do
need to keep a few basics in.

I am using cooked and
smoked salmon, but sausage
sliced up would be good, or
if you prefer no meat or fish
just use different cheeses
and onions.

The most important part
of this is the use of a block
of puff pastry.

I am a baker and have the
skills to make puff pastry.

However, there are some
convenience foods that are
well worth using and shop-
bought puff pastry is one of
them, especially the all-
butter version.

*Pre-heated oven: Gas 6, 400f,
200c, 180 fan*

Ingredients

1 block of thawed puff
pastry;
1 tub of mascarpone cheese;
1-2 cloves of crushed garlic;

50g grated parmesan or
shavings;
3 spring onions;
150g of cooked salmon/

Summat Quick F'Tea

smoked salmon or a
combination of both;
plenty of freshly milled
black pepper and salt

Method
Roll out the puff pastry until
it is the size of an A4 sheet
of paper. After which, tidy

the edges and lay it on a baking sheet.

Prick the pastry with a folk and, if you wish, cut an inch edge all around, but making sure you only cut halfway through.

Prick the centre well, so that it does not rise too much.

Chill the pastry on the baking sheet for at least 30 minutes before baking in a pre-heated oven.

Alternatively, roll out the pastry and lay it on the baking sheet. Cover it with a sheet of greaseproof paper and lay another baking sheet on top.

In this way the pastry rises but not too much, the result being a crisp thin base perfect for a tart as a buffet dish or tasty supper. Chill for 30 minutes.

Bake the sheet of pastry for about 10 minutes until it is half done.

To bake to full brownness would lead to the tart being over-baked. Once the topping has had a chance to heat up, cook.

While the pastry is cooking, put the mascarpone garlic and seasoning in a dish and mix well, add in the parmesan and spring onions, saving one spring onion for use on the top).

Remove the tart from the oven and take off the top baking sheet.

The base can be made in advance and topped from cold.

Spread the top of the tart with the mascarpone and onions mixture, then top with the flaked salmon, fresh spring onion, sliced mushrooms, grated cheese or whatever you fancy.

Some tartar sauce would be lovely mixed into the mascarpone base, or use a little chilli if you are topping with sliced sausage.

Bake for about 15 minutes or until the topping is bubbling and brown. Serve with a chopped salad.

WHITBY CHOWDER

One of my top 10 places in the world, Whitby has a warm, friendly feel and is steeped in history.

The town dates to Roman times. Near the Abbey are the remains of one of their lighthouses, the Saxons calling the town Streonshal, meaning lighthouse bay.

Whitby is famous not only for its fabulous fish, but also that deep rich shiny black stone Whitby Jet, which is fossilised monkey puzzle tree, made famous by Queen Victoria who wore the black jewel during her mourning for Prince Albert.

Whitby influenced many people throughout history, one being Bram Stoker, who they say was captivated by the crashing waves and majestic cliffs when writing *Dracula*.

One of the most famous sons of the area was Captain James Cook, who set sail as an apprentice at the age of 18 and later went on to explore, Newfoundland, Australia, New Zealand and Hawaii; if you're lucky you may be in town when a replica of his ship *Endeavour* sails into the natural harbour.

This is a great feast of a dish, not tricky to make, and can be tweaked to your exact taste.

How I make it sometimes depends on what I have in for the vegetable base. I often use the soup pack of fresh veg the supermarkets have already prepared.

Use something like the leek and potato soup mix.

If you are not a fish lover then replace the fish stock cube with a chicken or vegetable one and put in chunks of chicken in place of the fish. Or you can leave it as just vegetable chowder.

Serves 4 hungry people or 6 as a starter.

Whitby Chowder

Ingredients

Approximately 500g finely diced veg, include onion, leek, peeled potato, carrot; 200g diced smoked bacon (lardons or pancetta – if you don't want to use bacon replace with 2 table spoons of oil and 50g butter); 2–3 cloves of crushed garlic; 500mls of water; 500mls of whole milk (it must be whole or even better the real creamy milk); 1 fish stock cube (the jelly type);

200ml white wine; 2-3 teaspoons of chopped parsley (fresh or dried); plenty of freshly ground black pepper; salt to taste; 500g fish, (it is always best to have a mix of one white firm fish such as cod or haddock, one red fish such as salmon or trout, and one smoked fish such as smoked haddock); ¼ pint double cream (optional)

Method

In a large heavy-bottomed pan, fry the bacon until it gives of some oil and starts to brown. If not using bacon heat the oil and butter, add the chopped vegetables and sauté until starting to soften but not brown.

Add in the garlic and the stock cube and 200ml of white wine, plus the 500ml water to dissolve the stock in, and to start to cook the vegetables.

Allow this all to simmer on a very low heat until the veg is soft. (If you need a little more liquid to cook the vegetables and bacon add a bit more wine or water.)

Add milk but do not use all the milk at this stage; save about 200mls to let the chowder down later if it's too thick. This will depend on how much potato you decide to use.

A word about the potato;

it will thicken the chowder but if you use too much there is a tendency for the chowder to become too 'gloopy and grainy'.

Simmer and taste the chowder using as much salt, pepper and garlic as you like. Go steady with the salt as there could be quite a bit in the smoked fish.

Do not let the chowder boil as this may split the milk. If the milk in the chowder looks like it has curdled just whisk the mixture with a balloon hand whisk.

The light whisking helps to amalgamate the soft vegetables into the soup and thicken it, plus it helps to emulsify the overall chowder.

Cut the fish into bite size chunks and, when the soup is completely cooked and piping hot, take off the heat.

Gently stir in the fish and chopped parsley, put the lid on the pan and let the heat of the chowder cook the fish.

If the prospect of just the heat of the chowder cooking the fish worries you, then by all means place the fish in the oven and cook on a medium heat for no more than five minutes.

If you are making this ahead then make the chowder up to where the fish goes in.

Hold back from putting in the fish and when you are ready to serve heat the chowder until piping hot, but not boiling, then add in your fish and leave with the heat off but the pan lid placed tightly on.

If you are feeling decidely decadent, just before you put in the fish add ¼ pint of double cream for that added luxury.

This meal is best served with some crusty bread and butter, all the better to transport you to Whitby.

YORKSHIRE PUDDINGS

Where does one start to explain how to make the best Yorkshire pudding?

Is it a starter, a filler, a sweet pudding? All of those – and more?

Nibble them cold while washing up after dinner or make some because there is a plethora of gravy left over from some braised meat.

Yorkshire puddings are worth their weight in gold.

This makes about 24, bun-tin sized.

Pre-heated oven: Gas 8, 450f, 240c, 210 fan (if using a gas oven move the oven shelves to near the top of the oven for maximum heat)

Ingredients
200gms plain flour;
4 eggs;
250mls of milk (preferably whole milk);
pinch of salt;
50gms of lard, goose fat (oil if you don't eat meat) but the hard fat is best.

Method
Preferably make the batter a good few hours before you need it. This resting helps the puddings to rise.

If you don't have that amount of time, just try and give the mixture half an hour resting.

Crack the eggs into a bowl and sprinkle on the flour and salt.

Whisk these together, the batter will be quite thick and sticky, now gradually pour in the milk a bit at a time.

The size of the egg will determine how much milk is needed.

And in fact the eggs are more important than the milk, because eggs will help the puddings to rise.

Whisk until the mixture is the texture of unwhipped

65

Yorkshire Puddings

double cream. Pour this mixture into a jug with a good spout and leave to rest for as long as you can.

Thirty minutes before you need the puddings, it is time to pre-heat the oven.

To prepare the tins, put a touch of fat – 2g or the end of a knifeful – into each bun tin. Put the trays into the oven and leave for a 5–7 minutes until the fat is smoking hot.

Now comes the tricky bit, especially if you are wearing mascara as the heat of the oven will melt it!

My dad always taught me to take the jug of mixture to the oven, not to lift the tray away from the oven door, thus keeping the fat as hot as possible.

With the jug in one hand, open the oven door and with the bun tray just resting on the edge of the oven shelf, quickly pour about two tablespoons worth of batter on to the fat. You need to hear a sizzle as the batter hits.

There is no need to use a spoon, just splash out an amount from the jug.

Gently slide the bun tray back into the oven and wait. It is good to watch as your puddings rise and colour in front of your eyes, which could take about 15 minutes depending on the oven.

Once they are a good dark golden-brown, lift out and show as many people as you can or take photos of your creation as the air soon deflates out of the puddings.

Serve with lashings of gravy and be proud.

Then sit back and listen to the monologue for how the 'Best Yorkshire Puddin were Made', written by Stanley Holloway, easily available online.

"Hi waitress, excuse me a minute, now listen...
I'm not finding fault, but here, Miss...
The 'taters look gradely... the beef is a'reet...
But what kind of pudden is this....?"...

'TO FINISH WI"

A term used to describe desserts.

BAKEWELL TART

BIRSTALL PIE FILLING

BRONTË SOUFFLÉ

CRAVEN BUTTERCREAM

HELVELLYN BUTTER

ICE CREAM OF MANY COLOURS

MASHAM PANNA COTTA
WITH MOLASSES TOFFEE SAUCE

ROSEDALE GATEAUX

THAT 'DAM' TRIFLE

TUSKY CHEESECAKE

WASTE NOT WANT NOT TART

YORKIST TART

Bakewell Tart

BAKEWELL TART

It's always tricky putting your name against one of the classics, and I do this with the upmost respect for the town of Bakewell.

The question I often get asked is what is the difference between a Bakewell tart and a Bakewell pudding?

A Bakewell tart is a short pastry case with a layer of jam and a sponge with the addition of ground almonds, topped with fondant icing which is feathered or finished with a glacé cherry.

A Bakewell pudding is a case of buttery puff pastry followed by a layer of strawberry jam, then filled with soft set custard and incorporating sugar and almonds.

This is my humble version made in admiration of the classic.

Pre-heated oven: Gas 4, 350f, 180c, 160 fan
8in/20cm loose bottom flan tin

Ingredients

half the quantity of Best
Northern Short curst pastry
– see part 5;
3 tablespoons of jam of your
choice (I prefer raspberry);
100g soft margarine;
100g caster sugar ;
2 eggs;

80g self-raising flour;
50g ground almonds;
½ teaspoon of almond
extract.
Topping:
100g icing sugar;
1 tablespoon lemon juice;
touch of food colouring

Method

Roll out the pastry and line
a flan tin, (preferably one
with a loose bottom).

Leave an edge hanging
over which can be trimmed
off after the tart has baked.

Chill the tart case while
you are making the filling.

It's best to put the tart
case on a baking sheet to
catch any bits of pastry that
may break off during
cooking, it also helps to
brown the base of the tart.

To make the filling, cream
the margarine and sugar
together until light and
fluffy, add in the eggs and
mix well.

Fold in the flour and

ground almonds along with
the almond extract.

Spread the base of the tart
case with the jam of your
choice.

Carefully spoon the
sponge mixture over the
jam, level the top and bake
in the oven for around 30–45
minutes depending on your
oven.

I've baked this tart a bit
slower so that it gives the
pastry time to cook and
brown.

While the pastry is
cooking make the icing.

Put the icing sugar in a
bowl and add the lemon
juice teaspoon by teaspoon.

You want the icing to be thick enough to hold, but runny enough to pour over the finished tart without tearing up the sponge, so ideally it needs to be the texture of runny honey.

Prepare to 'feather' the top of the tart.

Take about a tablespoon of your icing and, in a cup, add a touch of colouring gel. I like to use brown.

Pour this into a piping bag and nip off a tiny bit of the end to give you a trail about the width of a pencil lead.

When the tart has browned to a dark gold and the cake filling has cooked, remove from the oven and leave to cool.

Using a serrated knife trim the edges of the tart and remove the overhang of pastry to give a tidy edge.

Leave the tart to cool completely before removing from the tart case.

Pour the white icing over the top and spread to the edge of the tart. While this icing is wet, pipe several lines of the coloured icing across it.

Then, using a cocktail stick, lightly drag the pick across the line of coloured icing and the white, reverse about 2cms from your first row and pull the cocktail stick back down the tart, repeat this until you have come to the end of the tart.

This feathering effect is quite easy to do and looks fabulous!

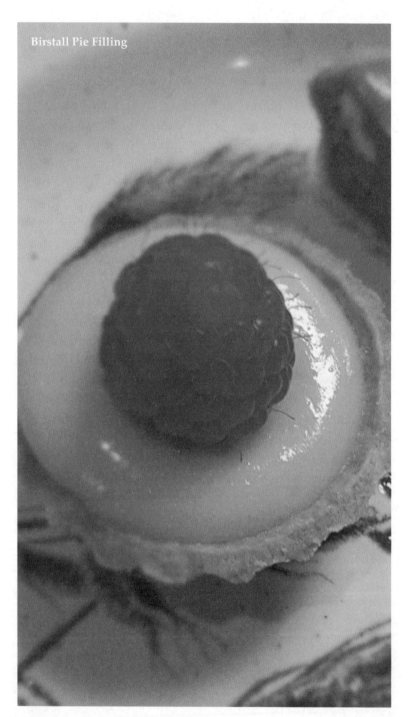

Birstall Pie Filling

BIRSTALL PIE FILLING

This is perfect for combining a Yorkshire invention with the juicy, succulent taste of Mediterranean citrus.

Joseph Priestley, born in Birstall, near Batley, was one of three men credited with the discovery of oxygen, the other two being Carl Scheele and Antoine Lavoisier.

Nevertheless, it is certain that good old Joe invented carbonated water.

Then in 1871, from his home in Huddersfield, Ben Shaw sold herbal water from his horse and cart and went on to create other fizzy favourites like dandelion and burdock (best beverage to have with fish and chips) and his unique lemonade.

I use this filling in so many ways... folding it into double cream and layering it with crushed ginger biscuits for a quick dessert.

Or filling sweet, pre-cooked tart cases topped with finished meringue for a dessert canapé.

And covering a larger pastry case topped with meringue for my all-time fave, lemon meringue pie. This is not a curd, more of a 'pudding 'style texture.

Ingredients
150mls lemon juice;
4 medium egg yolks;
2 medium whole eggs;
100g caster sugar;
100g soft unsalted butter

Method
Put the lemon juice, egg yolks, eggs, butter and sugar into a pan and whisk together.

Place over a low heat (do not leave the pan at this stage) and stir until the mixture become thick.

Pass the hot mixture through a sieve into a clean bowl. In this way, any cooked white of egg will be discarded.

Then, use the delicious lemon cream as shamelessly as you see fit.

Brontë Soufflé

BRONTË SOUFFLÉ

Soufflé comes from the French verb *souffler*, meaning to blow, to breathe, to inflate, or to puff.

Cast your imagination back to 1842, when two young ladies from Yorkshire set out to work as teachers in Brussels (which was part of France until 1815).

Charlotte and Emily Brontë, two of a trio of heroines who epitomise the tenacity and passion of so many of us northern lasses, also went there to acquire an education themselves.

Then, having returned from Belgium, they went on to write stories and poetry destined to steal the hearts of the world.

In Charlotte's case, *The Professor* and *Villette* were particularly influenced by those experiences abroad.

And having embedded themselves in the culture, it is easy to imagine how they might have sat down to the exotic delicacy, enjoyed it, and brought it back to their parsonage, surrounded by the majestic, dark and haunting moors of Haworth.

Another one of my dearest mum's recipes, this is a cheeky, easy to make but impressive soufflé.

If you make a tin foil cuff and secure it around the top of a soufflé dish you will end up with that gratifying look of the dessert being higher than the dish.

My parents were great at entertaining.

Growing up in the 1970s, I used to love watching what fresh culinary delights my mum could come up with for her guests.

This was once such.

You will need a hand or stand whisk for this recipe, as outlined overleaf.

Part 3

Ingredients

1 lemon jelly;
½ pint hot water;
100g dark chocolate;
1 large can evaporated milk
(chilled);
50g dark chocolate strands
or other small decorations
(chopped nuts, flaked
almonds etc or coco powder);
7in soufflé dish or 6
individual ramekins;
6cm deep strip of tin foil
(double thickness) length of
the circumference of the
dish with 3cm extra, plus
some tape.

Method

Prepare the soufflé dish or individual ramekins if you prefer by wrapping the tin foil around the top edge.

Tape the paper in place, remembering to place some around the base, securing it to the dish.

Break the jelly into cubes and place in a jug. Pour on the boiling water and stir until dissolved.

While the jelly is cooling, start to whip the tin of chilled evaporated milk (cold milk will whip much quicker). Whisk until thick and creamy. This could take 5-10 minutes.

When the jelly is cool pour it into the whipped milk and continue to whisk until well combined.

Leave the jelly in the mixing bowl to start to set. Meanwhile, melt the chocolate in bowl set over a pan of simmering water.

Once the jelly mixture is on the point of setting and, while the mixer is running on low, pour in the melted chocolate.

It should only take a few seconds to combine.

Carefully pour the mixture into the soufflé dish making sure not to catch the foil cuff. Fill up past the edge of the dish and into the cuff area. Carefully put it into the fridge and leave to go cold and set.

The height of the soufflé will depend on the size of the soufflé dish.

The smaller the dish the higher the soufflé sits above it. Alternatively, make the soufflé, serve in a beautiful glass dish and call it mousse.

Carefully peel off the foil and this will leave you with a rough side, which can be left if you just want to decorate the top with swirls of whipped cream (very retro).

Or you could carefully fill the palm of one hand with chocolate strands, flaked almonds or cocoa powder, and gently press this onto this rough edge.

Turn the soufflé with the other hand. Do this until you have covered all the exposed edge.

Serve with pouring cream. You could make this with white chocolate and maybe a blackcurrant jelly.

CRAVEN BUTTERCREAM

During the 1920s, a group of Yorkshire dairy farmers joined forces to form Hindell's Dairy Farmers Ltd.

This was, in the main, to stabilise the cost of milk and dairy. Later, in 1949, Arthur Stockdale, a Yorkshireman himself, became MD for the re-named Associated Dairies and Farm Stores Ltd.

During the 1950s and 60s Associated Dairies expanded and introduced several pork butchers and the brand 'Craven Dairies', which covered their cake shops.

Arthur's son, Noel, followed in his father's footsteps at Associated Dairies. He had some very good friends, Peter and Fred Asquith, who were butchers with around seven shops.

They went on to become ASDA (Asquith and Dairies). Thus history was made here in the north!

This is a fabulous find. If you want a change from regular buttercream then give it a whirl.

It's very easy to concoct, however you do need to adhere to the instructions carefully.

Once made it can be flavoured with coffee, chocolate, caramel, or just gorgeous vanilla.

This recipe does really need an electric hand whisk or stand mixer.

Ingredients
500g soft but not melted butter (room temperature); 250g white vegetable fat such as Trex; 1 large can of chilled condensed milk (379g)

Method
Beat the butter and white vegetable fat together on high speed for a good five minutes.

The butter needs to be very light in colour, fluffed up and voluminous.

Pour in the tin of chilled condensed milk and whisk for a good 2-3 minutes until the mixture is smooth and stable. Use as you would other buttercreams.

This is great to pipe on buns, between layer cakes, under fondant for celebration cakes etc.

Flavourings
Chocolate: Melt 200g of good quality chocolate, (milk, dark or white). While it is still warm, pour into the buttercream and beat for two minutes.

Coffee: 2 teaspoons of good instant coffee (espresso powder); 2 teaspoons of hot water to dissolve. Pour on to buttercream and beat (add when the coffee mixture has cooled).

Caramel: Use tinned caramel in place of the condensed milk. This will have to be spooned in while the mixer is on a slow speed.

Vanilla: 1 teaspoon of vanilla bean paste (buttercream looks amazing with the tiny vanilla seeds).

Craven Buttercream

Helvellyn Butter

HELVELLYN BUTTER

Here's something we use mainly at Christmas on top of hot Christmas pudding and warm mince pies.

One considered origin of what we now know as brandy butter derives from Cumbria, where it was made mainly using rum.

In America, brandy or rum butter is known as 'hard sauce'.

Cumbria forms an idyllic and breathtaking part of the north of England, within which is the Lake District.

And majestically within that stands the third highest mountain in England – Helvellyn – at a towering 3,120 feet.

In 1926, a small plane landed on the summit of Helvellyn. When taking off again, the plane nearly crashed, just missing Striding Edge.

There is a stone marking this event on the summit.

One of the most famous portraits of the poet William Wordsworth, painted by Benjamin Robert Hayton, has him on the mountainside with Helvellyn in the background, a hard mountain to climb, from where rum butter originates!

Back to the brandy butter.

This treasure comes, as do all my most precious recipes, from my mum. No matter how busy she was and nor how late it got on Christmas Eve, this brandy butter was made and ready for the day.

It really is a delectable combination of butter, egg, ground almonds and double cream.

It is best served frozen, with a dreamy blob melting on warm pudding.

This is especially cheeky and delightful when eaten not straight after Christmas dinner, but around 11pm, when the house is quiet, and you are sitting up late watching a favourite festive film.

Ingredients
50g butter (soft);
100g soft brown sugar;
1 egg yolk (very fresh as it is not going to be cooked);
50g ground almonds;
2 tablespoons of brandy;
200mls double cream

Method
Cream the soft butter and sugar together until light and fluffy, beat in the egg and ground almonds.

Add in brandy or rum and taste. Whip the double cream until it just falls soft, fold this into the butter, egg and brandy mixture. It will be quite soft at this stage. Chill in the fridge until firm then pile high into a serving dish and freeze.

Best served straight from the freezer. Be a little wary that too much spirit could be overbearing and bitter.

The beauty of this recipe is that it is delicious on its own and has a subtlety that enhances the main pudding.

This is ideal to make a double batch and freeze into decorative pots for gifts.

ICE CREAM OF MANY COLOURS

This is the easiest ice cream you will come across.

I use it all the time, just change flavours depending on how I want to serve it.

You can use a jar of tangy lemon curd or make it with chopped crystalized ginger.

Sweet mince pie ice cream is lovely and one of my favourites is liquorice ripple. An acquired taste but, still, it works well.

Ice cream base ingredients
1 large tin of condensed milk;
1 pint of double cream;
1 teaspoon vanilla extract.

Method
Combine all the ingredients together.

If you prefer a lighter ice-cream just whip the ingredients until it forms soft peaks.

Fold in the flavourings

Mince pie: 3 heaped tablespoons of good quality mincemeat; 4 crumbled up shortbread biscuits. (I think this works better than using broken actual mince pies)

Liquorice ripple: A true taste of Yorkshire. 200g of Pontefract cakes in a pan with 150mls of water, place over a low heat and melt slowly, stirring occasionally.

If the mixture becomes too thick add another 2 tablespoons of water.

When this mixture has melted (don't worry about the odd chuck of Pontefract cake, it just adds to the texture) allow it to cool and stir it into the into the basic

Ice Cream of Many Colours

ice cream mixture. It may be wise to pour the basic ice-cream into the freezer container and then pour on the liquorice using the back of a knife to swirl it together.

This is the best way to obtain the 'ripple' effect.

Once the containers have been filled, put on the lid and freeze, no need to keep churning and checking.

For the best result, I would take the ice-cream out of the freezer 30 minutes before you need it. Serve either on its own or as an addition to other desserts.

The liquorice ripple is especially gorgeous with a slice of chocolate tart.

Ideas: Split the basic mixture and make two smaller batches to combine complementary flavours, eg ginger and orange – chopped crystallised ginger and the zest of 2 large oranges or mint choc chip – 4 teaspoons of mint extract (always use extract never essence), 200g chopped chocolate (the darker the better), 1-2 drops of green food colouring.

By no means is this list exhaustive and please don't be governed by the amounts I have given. Put in as much or as little as you like. Just make sure you enjoy and share your creations with as many people as you can.

Masham Panna Cotta
with mollasses toffee sauce

MASHAM PANNA COTTA
WITH MOLASSES TOFFEE SAUCE

Tucked into a corner of Wensleydale is the ancient town of Masham, originally known for its sheep farming which was introduced by invading Vikings after they burnt the church down.

Those pesky Vikings gave with one hand and took away with the other.

However, sheep farming put the town on the map and in later years it hosted the largest market square in the region due to its wealth of sheep helped by the nearby Abbeys of Jervaulx and Fountains.

The town holds an annual sheep fair in September which is well attended not only for the livestock but because of its two breweries that sit happily next door to one another.

Theakston's and Black Sheep both produce awarding winning beer. I have chosen to use Black Sheep Milk Stout for this panna cotta, but please try some of the other craft porters produced in this fine town.

This dessert is one of those puddings worth a try for a dinner party, it is subtle and sophisticated.

The sauce is a different story, everyone will love it and pour it over whatever they can find, be aware of someone stood with the fridge door open, teaspoon in hand eating set sauce out of the jug!

I have made the sauce with molasses sugar, but you can use a lighter soft brown sugar.

When I first tried this recipe, I used eight sheets of gelatine and, to be honest, you could have used it as a trampoline. However, after trial and error I found that less gelatine gives a softer set thus a more luxurious dessert.

Ingredients

1 pint double cream;
¼ pint milk (full fat);
200mls milk stout
(Black Sheep milk stout);
4 sheets gelatine;
toffee sauce;

200mls double cream;
100g unsalted butter;
100g brown sugar
(molasses, soft brown or
dark brown)

Method

Put the gelatine sheets in
cold water to soften, set to
one side.

Put the cream, milk and
stout in a pan, warm gently,
do not let the mixture boil.
Take the mixture off the heat
to cool slightly.

Squeeze the excess water
out of the gelatine sheets
and drop them into the
cream and stout mixture.

Gently pour the cream
and stout mixture into
separate ramekins or small
dishes, alternatively pour
the mixture into a pretty
glass serving dish.

Place in the fridge and
allow to set. This will take
from two to four hours
depending on the size of the
dish/dishes.

To make the sauce, melt
the butter and sugar
together in a pan over a low
heat. Once the sugar has
dissolved and the mixture is
bubbling add cream and stir.

Keep stirring and boiling
until the sauce is the colour
and thickness you like.

It will thicken as it cools,
so I'd suggest just boil until
it is a rich nutty colour.

To serve, if you have
made small ramekins pour a
pool of cool sauce over the
panna cotta and serve –
make sure the sauce is cool
enough not to melt the
cream.

Alternatively serve the
sauce in a jug with the
larger panna cotta for
people to help themselves.

ROSEDALE GATEAUX

Spinach is packed with iron and so are the North Yorkshire Moors.

A hive of activity 150 years ago, during the industrial revolution, they were being mined to build railways and industrial machinery.

The Whitby and Pickering railway would transport iron ore to other construction sites cutting through the Rosedale and Esk valley, further routes would take the iron to Teesside and the world.

This cake may sound somewhat different but, believe me, it is delicious.

It does not taste of spinach. It is just the most fabulous colour and so incredibly moist.

It does have a few components, but works as a celebration cake. I would suggest you go to town on decoration and presentation.
Pre-heated oven: Gas 5, 375f, 190c, 170 fan

Ingredients
3 eggs;
1 teaspoon vanilla;
200g caster sugar;
200g washed fresh spinach leaves;
200mls rape seed oil;
juice of one large lemon;
325g self-raising flour;
½ teaspoon salt;
½ teaspoon baking powder

Filling ingredients
lime butter cream;
100g very soft butter or margarine;
300g icing sugar;
juice of one lime;
grated zest of 3 limes;
minted frosting;
1 large can evaporated milk
200g sugar;
350g dark chopped chocolate;
peppermint extract (3–5 teaspoons depending on taste)

Method
Place the eggs, sugar, vanilla, and spinach in a

Rosedale Gateaux

blender or food processor. Blitz all the ingredients until they are smooth.

Pour in the oil while the motor is running.

Sift flour, salt and baking powder together, pour in the flour gradually down the funnel of the processor as it runs. Let the mixture combine for a few seconds. Pour into two lined and greased 7in sandwich tins.

Bake in a pre-heated oven for approximately 25 minutes depending on oven

Filling

Using an electric mixer, beat the soft butter and icing sugar together until light and fluffy. Mix in the grated zest and just enough of the lime juice to dissolve the sugar. Add a teaspoon at a time otherwise you will need to add more icing sugar.

Minted frosting

Put sugar and evaporated milk in a medium-sized pan.

Slowly bring to the boil, it will quickly boil over so

turn the heat down and simmer for six minutes.

Meanwhile, break the chocolate or weigh out the chocolate chips. Take the milk and sugar off the heat and stir in the chocolate.

Keep stirring until smooth and shiny, cool with the pan lid on to prevent a skin from forming.

Decorating

This is entirely up to you. There are two frostings and two cakes.

You can split the cakes and fill with the lime butter cream, then cover the whole cake with the minted frosting.

Or fill the cake with the minted frosting and cover the cake with the lime butter cream.

You could make the cake in tray bake style and just cover the top with either of the frostings and serve in squares. How about putting the mint in the buttercream and the lime zest in the chocolate frosting?

That 'Dam' Trifle

THAT 'DAM' TRIFLE

Finding a northern link to my tiramisu had me stumped for a while, but while walking round Yeadon Dam or Yeadon Tarn or Yeadon Moor Dam every morning I suddenly had this light bulb moment!

Yeadon is an Anglo-Saxon name meaning 'water on the hill', there has always been some natural water hole at the top of the town.

Over the years the dam has been enlarged for industrial purposes and improved for leisure use.

In 1925, Yeadon District Council bought the dam from Messrs D Waterworth for the sum of £2,400, and in 1935 stones were put round it to prevent erosion. During the war the dam was drained as the enemy knew that the Avro factory was situated close to water. They contributed to the making of 700 Lancaster Bombers and 4,500 Ansons before decommissioned in around 1947. Apparently, film star Gracie Fields came to entertain the workers.

This place is my home. I grew up at one side, moved to the top side and returned to the other side, the only place I haven't lived is the bottom side, but that one is the runway to Leeds Bradford Airport or 'Yeadon Airport' as it's best known.

A great party pudding, it can be made ahead. In fact, this is best made a couple of days before and kept in the fridge.

You can make the sponge fingers yourself, but sometimes life is a bit too short and we want the delicious finished dessert as soon as possible.

There are a few parts to making this, but having done it once you'll soon have them down to a fine art. I am a big advocate of having a pudding like this for breakfast!

Part 3

Ingredients

Two packets sponge fingers (you may need only a few out of the second packet); 3 very fresh free range eggs (separated); 2 x 300g tubs of mascarpone cheese; ¼ pint very strong black coffee; ¼ pint of masala wine; 200g caster sugar; 50g cocoa powder for dusting the top

Method

Choose a presentation dish.

I use a white 10 x 12cm one, but you could use a glass one, so that the layers can be seen.

Make up the coffee. When cold add in half the masala wine.

Whisk the egg yolks with the sugar until thick and creamy, then fold in the mascarpone cheese and whisk again until there are no lumps of cheese.

Whisk the egg whites until they form soft peaks. Using one spoonful of whites, whisk this into the cheese mixture (this slackens the mixture making it easier to fold in the rest of the whites carefully).

Dip each sponge finger into the coffee and masala and arrange in the bottom of the dish.

When you have a neat and tightly filled dish, spoon on half the cheese mixture.

Dip the rest of the sponge fingers in the coffee and masala and lay on top of the second layer, repeat with the rest of the cheese mixture.

The whole thing will look a bit messy at this stage, but in time the sponge fingers will soak up the liquid.

Leave in the fridge to chill for as long as you can, but definitely overnight.

Just before serving, dredge the top with cocoa.

TUSKY CHEESECAKE

Tusky being the Yorkshire word for rhubarb, and Yorkshire – specifically the Rhubarb Triangle – being the home of forced rhubarb, this cheesecake is a must!

Rhubarb is a native of Siberia, so our damp, cold winters and loamy soil offer ideal growing conditions.

The Wakefield, Morley Rothwell area has cultivated the specialist process of growing rhubarb in warm, dark sheds in candlelight forcing it into sweet tender stems renowned the world over and holding PDO (protective designation of origin).

The world of rhubarb is a fascinating and worth closer investigation – maybe while eating a slice of this delicious cheesecake.

This is quite an old recipe, it's a cheesecake but more of an everyday style cheesecake pie. It is not dissimilar to a curd tart but using cream cheese.

I have added rhubarb and ginger to this one, but it can be made with the addition of chopped peel, lemon zest and sultanas.

Please remember to roll the pastry as thin as you can. It is mainly there to hold the tart together, not to add much flavour.

As an optional extra I have added a thin layer of baked sour cream which adds a fantastic tangy edge. *Pre-heated oven: Gas 6, 400f, 200c, 180 fan*
This tart fills a deep 7in round flan case.

Ingredients – Pastry
200g self-raising flour;
100g butter;
1 egg and a little milk;
1 tablespoon icing sugar;
pinch of salt

Method
Rub the butter into the flour until it resembles fine breadcrumbs. Stir in the sugar and pinch of salt. Beat

Tusky Cheesecake

the egg with a tablespoon of milk and use this to bring the flour mixture together.

Don't pour it all in at once, depending on the size of the egg.

When the dough is soft, but still firm enough to roll, cover and chill.

When the dough has chilled for about 30 minutes roll out until very thin and carefully line the tart case.

Leave plenty of pastry hanging over the edge and chill again for 15 minutes.

Line case with grease-proof paper and bake blind for 10-15 minutes. Lift out the paper and bake again for 10 more minutes.

Using a serrated knife,

trim off the overhanging pastry thus leaving a tidy neat edge that sits at the top of the case.

Ingredients – filling
50g soft butter;
30g caster sugar;
2 eggs;
200g cream cheese

Method
Cream the butter and sugar until light and fluffy, add in the beaten egg and mix well.

Stir in cream cheese and balloon whisk until the mixture is smooth.

If you are using the peel and sultans add at this stage: zest of one lemon, 30g candid chopped peel and 30g sultanas. Mix into the cream cheese mixture and pour into the pastry case.

If you are using the rhubarb and ginger: Poach 150g young, pink 'forced' Yorkshire rhubarb in two tablespoons of water with two teaspoons of ground ginger. Once the water and ginger have boiled add the chopped rhubarb and let it sit in the hot water, this is enough to poach the tender stems. Remove the rhubarb and drain on kitchen paper.

Finely chop crystallised ginger and add this to the cream cheese mixture. Lay rhubarb on the base of the baked case and pour over the cream cheese and ginger.

Bake for 25-30 minutes until the centre is set and top is light brown.

Optional topping: Mix 75ml -100ml of sour cream with 25g of caster sugar.

Once baked, gently pour the cream over the top but be careful as you pour not to break the top of the pie, it is best to do it from a spoon.

When the top is covered return to oven and bake for no longer than five minutes.

Cool the tart completely and place in the fridge before serving. Other fillings can be used, try chopped apricots or a thin layer of apricot puree on the bottom of the pastry case.

Waste Not Want Not Tart

WASTE NOT WANT NOT TART

In times gone by, most small holdings would have had a cow and, more often than not, made a small amount of cheese for themselves.

The by-product is curd and being true to the ethos that Yorkshire folk are frugal, nothing would go to waste, so the curd tart was born, after all, 'waste not want not' as they say here.

Curd tart is one that must be eaten before you tell someone what's in it!

Curds can be made quite easily by heating two pints of full fat milk to 37c/100f, remove from the heat and add three tablespoons of lemon juice. Leave it to curdle for about 10 minutes.

Spoon curds into a sieve lined with muslin or clean cotton handkerchief, leave to drain. Then use curds for the tart and whey to make scones or soda bread.

I've made this tart with either a combination of curds and ricotta or replace the curds with cottage cheese. I found that the ricotta made the tart creamy, especially left overnight. Next day, it was rich and sumptuous.

Pre-heated oven: Gas 4, 350f, 180c, 160 fan
This makes an 8in shallow pie plate or 6in deep tart case.

Ingredients
Use half quantity of 'The Best Northern Short Crust Pastry' – see part 5

Filling
150g fresh curd cheese (or made up of a combination from options above);
50g soft unsalted butter;
50g caster sugar;
1 large egg (beaten);
½ teaspoon mixed spice;
1 teaspoon freshly grated nutmeg (or more if you prefer);
50g currants (soaked in the juice of a lemon or orange along with the grated zest, ideally overnight).

Method

Roll out the pastry and line the pie plate or flan tin, leaving a slight overhang (this can be trimmed once the tart is cooked, it helps to give that sharp tidy edge)

Cream the butter and sugar in a bowl until light a fluffy, beat in the egg. Gradually fold in the fruit, lemon and curd mixture, mix well until there are no large lumps of curds.

Pour into the case and bake until the pastry is golden brown and the filling is 'tanned' and set, this usually takes about 30 to 40 minutes depending on your oven.

With a serrated knife, trim the pastry if it needs it. Leave to cool completely or, if you can, again overnight, the flavour and texture will improve as a result.

Yorkist Tart

YORKIST TART

When we think of chocolate we think of Rowntree's, Cadbury and Fry.

In the Victorian era these manufactures of chocolate and sweets were the largest in the country. York was fortunate to have a Quaker called Henry Isaac Rowntree who set up a factory in 1862.

Demand saw it soon grow, taking over an old iron foundry at Tanners Moat. Soon the business needed a new injection of cash and the Henry's brother became a partner.

Joseph Rowntree was an industrialist and believed in a happy work force, giving the workers' significant rights and privileges. The business now thriving moved to Haxby Road on

the outskirts of York in 1890. Rowntree's was bought by Nestlé in 1988 and slowly production of some of their best-known brands moved out of the country.

This not the easiest tart to make, but take care and persevere and you will have a delight to be proud of.

Be careful with the slices because, as much as we in the north are somewhat over generous with our portions, this tart does not need large slices. Much better if your guests go back for a second one.

Decorations are optional. What you use is not set in stone. Chocolate curls, fresh raspberries, strawberries dipped in chocolate would look amazing, or just a plain slice of deliciousness with a drizzle of single cream.

Perfection!

Pre-heated oven: Gas 5, 375f, 190c, 170 fan

Ingredients for the chocolate pastry
175gms plain flour;
½ teaspoon baking powder;
50gms cocoa;
50gms icing sugar;
140gms unsalted butter;
3 egg yolks

For the Filling
300gms 70% plain chocolate;
200gms milk chocolate;
200mls whole milk;
350mls double cream;
3 whole eggs;
2 tablespoons of camp coffee (optional)

To decorate (*optional*)
200gms white chocolate;
100gms freeze dried cherries

Method

Reduce the oven to: Gas 1, 275f, 140c, 120 fan to cook the filled flan.

Make the pastry using the Hollywood Chocolate Pastry recipe in part five, allowing it to chill.

Meanwhile, line a flat baking tray with parchment paper, butter a tart ring and put this on the lined tray.

Roll out the chocolate pastry between two sheets of cling film.

Peel off the top layer of cling film and gently lower the dough into the flan ring, using the cling film to guide.

Press gently into place and leave an overhang of pastry. Make sure there are no holes. Peel off the cling film and put a piece of parchment inside the flan case, fill with baking beans.

Bake for 15 minutes, remove the paper and beans and bake again for a further 10 minutes.

Remove and leave to cool on the tray. Trim off the excess pastry.

To make the decorations

(*optional*): Melt the white chocolate and spread thinly onto a flat clean tray, sprinkle on the crushed cherries and leave to set.

To make the filling:

Gently melt the chocolate in a bowl over a pan of barely simmering water.

In another pan, gently heat the cream and milk together with two tablespoons of camp coffee if you are using it.

In another bowl lightly whisk the eggs.

When the milk has heated pour it onto the egg whisking all the time. This becomes a custard.

Once the chocolate has melted, take it off the heat and placing a sieve over the bowl of chocolate, pour the custard onto it.

This process removes any cooked egg that may have formed a 'lump' and gives you a silky-smooth finish. Gently whisk the mixture until it turns chocolatey.

Carefully pour the mixture in the pastry case and bake in the oven for approximately one hour or until just set in the middle.

Remove from the oven and allow to cool completely.

Slide onto a serving plate using a large spatula.

This is the trickiest part of the whole dish; the best approach is to leave the ring on until the last minute and use a spatula that is large enough to cover the bottom of the tart.

Alternatively bake the whole tart in a loose bottom tart case and serve it by lifting off the side and leaving the base of the tin under the tart.

(No-one will ever know)

Decorations:

Using a metal scraper or palette knife, push it through the cold set white chocolate to make random curls and shavings. Alternatively, break the white chocolate into shards.

When the tart is cold, arrange the white chocolate decorations.

'BIT 'O' LUSH'

*A term used by Uncle Alex to describe
a cake, bun or biscuit.*

12 IN 12 OATIES

A1 COOKIES - THE GREAT NORTH COOKIE

ALLOTMENT BUNS

BATLEY TRUFFLE

BEDTIME MALT(ON) BISCUITS

BENTHAM BARS

BRAD EN BURG

CHAPELTOWN SLICE

GONGOOZLER'S SLICE

HARROGATE COFFEE AND WALNUT CAKE

'LITTLE SISTERS' CHERRY AND WALNUT COOKIES

NHS SHORTBREAD

OTLEY SALAMI

SLY CAKE DATE PASTRY

SOLDIERS CRISP

12 in 12 Oaties

12 IN 12 OATIES

My very good friends at Est Display, Jane and Tess, helped me so much on my *GBBO* journey.

They've printed labels, T-shirts and banners for me, we worked in collaboration on my first book and I own them my gratitude. They are also both very involved in getting people active and set up 12 in 12.

The aim is to undertake a regular fitness activity each month for a year, helping people stay active by making it a routine. They never leave their clients to struggle and can often be seen running around West Yorkshire, specifically under the runway of Leeds Bradford Airport with an army of keep fitters.

They asked me to help create a 'flapjack' style bar which would include honey from the bees they keep.

Pre-heated oven: Gas 4, 350f, 180c, 160 fan

Ingredients
150g self-raising wholemeal flour and a pinch of salt;
200g rolled oats;
50g dark brown sugar;
150g honey (or golden syrup, black treacle, molasses);
200g margarine
Fillings: 150g combination of sultanas, coconut, raisins, chocolate chips or similar;
Melted chocolate on top.

Method
Grease 35cm x 9cm flan tin. Place flour, oats and salt in a baking bowl, add fruit or other ingredients, mix well.

In a pan melt margarine, sugar and honey/syrup. Once melted but not boiling pour over the oats and flour, mix well to combine.

Press the mixture into tin, place on a baking sheet and bake for 20–25 minutes until the top is golden brown.

Leave to cool in the tin for 10 minutes then turn out onto a wire rack and cool completely.

Part 4

A1 COOKIES – THE GREAT NORTH COOKIE

The A1 that parallels the old Great North Road is one of the major routes bringing people to the region.

It runs for approximately 410 miles and is the longest numbered road in the UK.

These cookies are great if you want to make a large batch, perhaps for a long journey.

I often split the mixture after stage three and mix two combinations, for example, one half 250g plain chocolate chips, the other 250g combined white chocolate and cranberries.

Using ice cream scoops gives you the size of cookie.

Or how about making ice cream sandwiches – ice cream sandwiched between two chocolate and hazelnut cookies – yum!

There's no turning back from this one...

Pre-heated oven: Gas 5, 375f, 190c,170 fan
Ungreased baking trays

Ingredients
350g soft margarine;
200g granulated sugar;
200g soft brown sugar;
1 teaspoon vanilla extract;
2 eggs beaten;
pinch of salt;
650g self-raising flour;
2 teaspoons bicarb of soda;
500g of chocolate chips/nuts /dried fruit or combination

Method
Cream margarine and sugar. Add in beaten egg, vanilla and salt. Fold in all the dry ingredients sifted. Stir in nuts, fruit etc.

Using ice cream scoop to ensure biscuits are the same size, scoop onto baking tray, leaving a space between as these cookies do spread.

Bake in a pre-heated oven for about 15 minutes until set around the edges, but a bit soft in the middle. For a crisper cookie bake for a few more minutes. Leave on tray a while to firm up before transferring to a rack.

A1 Cookies –
The Great North Cookie

Allotment Buns

ALLOTMENT BUNS

In Anglo Saxon times, land was given to the labouring poor to grow their own food, thereby starting the idea of an allotment.

Hundreds of years later, due to growing populations and little or no welfare state, authorities were obliged by law to follow suit.

By 1908, local councils had to provide them according to demand and, by 1925, 250sqm was the average size of a plot.

From my childhood, I can remember raspberries growing on allotments, and being allowed to pick them would always end up with more being eaten than got taken home.

I grew up with raspberry buns, walking in to find a batch on the table and my mum busy with the next lot using another jam or curd – happy days.

Pre-heat the oven to Gas 5, 375f, 190c,170 fan
Grease a baking tray

Ingredients
1 pinch salt;
200g self-raising flour;
100g butter;
100g caster sugar;
1 egg, beaten;
2 to 3 drops of almond;
extract or vanilla paste;
raspberry jam;
25g desiccated coconut (opt)

Method
In a bowl, mix together the salt and flour, then cut in the butter and rub between fingertips until the mixture resembles breadcrumbs.

Add sugar and coconut (if using) and mix well. Mix in egg until a dough forms, then divide mixture into 12. If the dough is too stiff this may be due to small eggs, add drop of milk to slacken.

Shape each into a bun and place on prepared tray. Make a well in centre of the bun with thumb. Bake in the preheated oven for 12 to 15 minutes until brown and risen. Allow to cool.

BATLEY TRUFFLES

Number 17 Whitaker Street Batley, an unassuming terrace house, was a hive of activity in 1853. It was home to Michael Spedding, founder of Fox's biscuits.

These truffles are made using crushed quality biscuits, are very easy to make and great for children to have a go at baking. The flavour can be changed by using ginger biscuits and chopped crystallised ginger.

They can also be rolled in different finishes; melted chocolate, chopped mint leaves mixed with sugar or toasted ground almonds, a hint of green food colouring.

Use a food processor to get the biscuits really fine.

Ingredients
1 large packet of bourbon biscuits;
½ tin of 'tinned caramel' – see part 5;
2 teaspoons of peppermint extract;
300g melted chocolate

Method
Blitz the biscuits in the food processor nearly to powder. Tip into a bowl and add the peppermint extract and caramel. Bind and mix until it is all well incorporated.

Using damp hands, roll a small amount of the mixture into balls. Place on a baking try with space between each one. When completed, place in the fridge to harden.

Meanwhile melt the chocolate gently over a pan of simmering water.

When the truffles are cold use a fork to push each one around melted chocolate.

Place coated chocolate on greaseproof paper. Being cold will help it set a little more quickly. Pile them high and serve with coffee.

Alternatives: Use ginger biscuits or in place of the peppermint use whisky.

How about shortcake biscuits and cherry rolled in ruby chocolate?

Batley Truffles

Bedtime Malt(on) Biscuits

BEDTIME MALT(ON) BISCUITS

I called these biscuits after the town of Malton in North Yorkshire.

Always a lovely place to visit, especially when taking a drive on the back roads to Scarborough, Malton hosts a few microbrewers who make malt extract as part of the beer process.

Malting is basically the germinating of barley to promote sprouting, just before the grain sprouts the process is halted which releases enzymes that are used in beer making.

The next process is called mashing to release sugars from the malted grain, the liquid produced is concentrated by heat to evaporate the water thus leaving malt extract.

Malt is a lovely product to work with and Malton a fabulous market town with lots of history, shops and cafes.

Malt has some excellent properties, B vitamins – especially B6 – are good at lowering cholesterol and helps with the absorption of insulin. They support a healthy mind thus leading to relaxed sleep.

My brothers and sister and I never left home in the winter without a spoonful of cod liver oil and malt inside us. I hated it!

But I love these biscuits, which are an excellent supper served with a glass of warmed milk.

Pre-heated oven: Gas 3, 325f, 170c, 150 fan
Grease or line baking sheets

Ingredients

125g butter;
100g sugar (I often reduce
the sugar by half for a less
sweet biscuit, bit more of an
acquired taste);
1 egg;
½ teaspoon bicarbonate of
soda;

½ teaspoon cream of tartar;
2 tablespoons golden syrup
(or black treacle for a darker
less sweet biscuit);
2 tablespoons malt extract;
500g plain flour

Method

Cream the butter and sugar until light and fluffy.

Add the lightly beaten egg along with the soda and cream of tartar. Mix in the syrup and the malt until well combined.

Add in the flour and work all together until a soft ball is created.

Wrap it in clingfilm or place on a plate with a bowl over the top and chill for at least an hour.

Roll out the chilled dough to about ¼ in/1cm thick, cut out using a fluted cutter.

Place the biscuits well-spaced out on a baking sheet and bake slowly for 15 to 20 minutes.

Makes about 50 biscuits.

BENTHAM BARS

The two-sided town of Bentham consists of the smaller town High Bentham and Low Bentham.

Bentham sits nestled between North Yorkshire and Lancashire on the edge of the River Wenning. It was known for its weaving from the 18th century, especially hosepipes from flax.

This bar is a change from Millionaires Shortbread, but no less delicious.

It's so called because of the double sides, just like the twin parts of the town.

Ingredients
1 packet ice cream wafers;
250g dark chocolate;
25g butter;
2 teaspoons golden syrup;
caramel filling;
1 tin of condensed milk;
50g butter;
2 tablespoons golden syrup or black treacle;
1 tablespoon peanut butter or other butters, for example almond (optional)

Method
Cover the bottom of a square cake tin or deep Swiss roll tin with foil.

Lay the wafers neatly on the base and cut to size, take them out of the tin and duplicate the size and amount. Put these to one side in two piles.

Melt the chocolate, butter and golden syrup in a bowl set over a pan of simmering water, stirring occasionally until it has all melted.

Using half the chocolate, pour it onto the foil and spread evenly over the bottom of the cake tin.

Re-lay the wafers onto the warm chocolate, put this to one side to cool and set.

Make the caramel – combine the condensed milk, butter and golden syrup in a pan.

On a medium heat stir until all melted together and the mixture starts to bubble and thicken. Stir and gently boil for 5 to 10 minutes

Bentham Bars

depending on how dark you want your caramel.

Take off the heat and stir in the peanut butter if you are using it.

Spread the caramel over the wafers and chocolate and lay the second layer of wafers on top.

Using the rest of the melted chocolate spread this evenly and gently over the top layer of the wafers.

Chill for 30 minutes at least. Remove from fridge and let it reach room temp for about 20 minutes before slicing into bars or triangles.

BRAD EN BURG

A combination of Battenberg and Bradford.

In its heyday, the city was a metropolis and the heart of a thriving textile industry. It was prosperous and renowned across the world for its wool manufacturing.

This prosperity brought many to the area, including German merchants who arrived in around 1850 settling and making a home for themselves in an area dubbed Little Germany.

They brought culinary specialties with them, one of which would have been the cake Battenberg.

Little Germany now hosts about 85 buildings, some listed. Remember to look up as some have a hidden architectural beauty.

I've made this with chocolate cake, coffee cake and walnut buttercream.

You can buy a special tin to make Battenberg in and that would be a lovely treat, but wait and see if you like making it before you invest.

You can of course make your own marzipan or you can buy a block.

Pre-heated oven: Gas 4, 350f, 180c, 160 fan
Grease and line a 12in x 8in deep Swiss roll tin

Ingredients

150g soft margarine;
100g caster sugar;
150g self-raising flour;
3 eggs;
50g cocoa;
3 teaspoons espresso coffee
powder;
1 teaspoon hot water;
walnut butter cream;
100g walnuts (ground into a
paste using a processor or
pestle and mortar);
50g soft unsalted butter;
200g icing sugar.
Outside – 1 block of white
marzipan (1kg)

Method

Put the margarine, sugar,
eggs and flour into a large
mixing bowl and beat well
together until soft.

Split the mixture into two
bowls. Mix the coffee with
the hot water and mix into
one half of the cake batter.

Mix the cocoa with hot
water (about a tablespoon)
to make a paste and mix this
into the other bowl of plain
cake mix.

Using the oblong cake tin
divide into two equal parts
going vertically using card
wrapped in foil (if you don't
have a Battenberg tin).

Spread the coffee cake in
one half and the chocolate
cake mixture in the other
half, level the top and bake
for about 20-25 minutes or
until the mixture springs
back. Leave for about 5
minutes in the tin to cool
then turn out onto a wire
rack to cool completely.

Filling: While the cake is
cooking and cooling make
the buttercream. Cream the
butter and icing sugar.

If the cream is too stiff
add a teaspoon of milk,
when the butter cream is
light and fluffy stir in the
walnut paste.

Assembly: Cut the cooled
cakes into bars, do this by
trimming off the edges and
diving the two halves of
cake equally.

Make sure you use the
same measurements for the
other cake. The length will

Brad En Burg

depend on the tin you have used, but I would suggest for ease of handling make the strips of cake no longer than 10cm in length.

Put a chocolate strip next to a coffee strip and then on top put a coffee strip on top of a chocolate one and vice versa.

Once happy with the layout gently spread a layer of butter cream on all four sides of each strip.

Roll out the marzipan to a rectangle that will wrap over all four bars of cake.

Make sure there is plenty of butter cream on all edges of the cake, place on the rolled-out marzipan make the stack of cakes really tidy then carefully fold over the marzipan covering the cake completely.

Trim off the edges and using the palm of your hand, mould the cake gently into shape.

Dust the top with a touch of caster sugar and you may want to crimp the top edges of the burg.

Allow the cake to stand for an hour to firm up. Slice and serve with coffee.

CHAPELTOWN SLICE

Such a diverse and interesting suburb of the city of Leeds, Chapeltown Moor, as it was once called, spanned around 300 acres of green fields and park land.

It was here, in around 1700, races and archery contests took place and one of the first cricket matches in Yorkshire was played between the 'Gentlemen of Yorkshire' and the 'Gentlemen of Sheffield'.

Leeds is noted for its carnival, being one of the oldest in Europe.

In 1967 Arthur France, a student at Leeds University and originally from Saint Kitts, developed the Leeds West Indian Carnival held in

Chapeltown Slice

Potternewton Park which sits next to Chapeltown. It brings vibrancy to West Yorkshire, one of the best loved events of the year.

From the late 1940s into the 60s Britain encouraged immigration from the commonwealth to fill the labour shortage; many were ex-servicemen from the Caribbean bringing with

them culinary delights the likes of which we had never seen; spices, yams, coconuts, mango... the list goes on.

I have chosen coconut in this old fashioned 'must try' recipe, adapted from my mum's handwritten book.

Pre-heated oven: Gas 3, 325f, 170c, 150 fan
Grease a Swiss roll tin

Ingredients
Base – 100g margarine;
2 tablespoons icing sugar;
200g plain flour;
pinch of salt.
Topping – 2 eggs;
150g caster sugar;

50g self-raising flour;
1 teaspoon vanilla extract;
75g sliced toasted almonds (or other nuts);
50g desiccated coconut;
50g chopped cherries

Method
In a large baking bowl rub together the ingredients for the base. When the mixture resembles fine breadcrumbs, transfer to the greased Swiss roll tin and press firmly until smooth.

Put to one side.

To make the filling, whisk the eggs and sugar until light, thick, creamy and

foamy. Stir in the flour nuts and cherries. Pour this mixture over the base and place on an oven tray.

Bake for 40-45 minutes or until top is golden brown and firm to the touch.

Remove and leave to cool in the tin before cutting into slices and cooling completely on a wire rack.

GONGOOZLER'S SLICE

A Gongoozler is someone who enjoys watching activity on the canals of the United Kingdom.

Here in the north we boast the steepest flight of locks in the country, The Five Rise Locks at Bingley, built in 1774. Five chambers and six gates allow barges to climb up the rolling hills of countryside.

Due to the complexities in operating the locks there has always been a full-time keeper to help the boatmen to operate the intricate system, what a fabulous job!

This recipe uses five cups and so associating it with what is a fabulous feat of engineering seemed apt.

It is a family favourite and so easy to make, the only caution being there is a tendency to devour the lot and have to make more.

By no means is it set in stone that you must use the ingredients below. Please feel free to swap the nuts, fruit or chocolate. You can make this as large or as small as you like depending on which cup you use.

Pre-heated oven: Gas 4, 350f, 180c, 160 fan
20cm x 30cm Swiss roll tin

Ingredients
1 cup sultanas;
1 cup chocolate bits –
we like dark best;
1 cup roasted peanuts (salted or unsalted is your choice);
1 cup desiccated coconut –

I prefer to use chopped mixed nuts here;
1 cup sweetened condensed milk;
either a Snickers or Mars bar (or both);
25g of butter/margarine

Gongoozler's Slice

Method

Line the Swiss roll tin with greaseproof paper – I use the foil which is lined with greaseproof paper when I have it.

In a bowl combine the fruit, nuts and chocolate, stir in the condensed milk and mix well.

Tip the mixture into the lined tray and press until level (I use damp hands to do this).

Cover the tray with foil and bake for about 20 mins. Take off the cover and bake for a further 10 mins. Leave to cool in the pan.

In a small pan melt together either a Snicker or a Mars Bar with 25g of butter/margarine. I find the ratio is 1:1 so if you do both bars use 50g. When melted to a runny goo – drizzle over the cooled slice.

When cool cut into small squares – it is very rich but lovely. Experiment with other dry ingredients, you are only limited by your imagination.

HARROGATE COFFEE AND WALNUT CAKE

The gorgeous and classy Spa town of Harrogate in North Yorkshire was from 2013-15 voted one of the happiest places to live in the UK.

That's due to its beautiful parkland and suave hotels – many commandeered for government offices fleeing war torn London during the Second World War.

Or maybe because Harrogate is the home of Taylors coffee, a family run company founded in 1886 which still produces some of the best ground coffee in the north.

Harrogate is also home of the famous Betty's tearoom which, in 1962, joined forces with Taylors.

This cake is modelled on something I can imagine in the window of Betty's, using Taylors rich aromatic coffee and possibly eaten by author Agatha Christie, who went missing from her home in 1926 and was found in The Old Swan Hotel, 11 days later, a stroll up Parliament Street.

I usually make it in a small roasting style tin or deep Swiss roll tin. It cuts into squares and is fabulous to use at a fate, school or church fair.

Another reason I love it so much is that it's made all in one bowl.

However, it relies on you giving the ingredients a good mixing with a wooden spoon for a couple of minutes because it needs the air that you would have put in during the conventional baking stages.

Pre-heated oven: Gas 4, 350f, 180c, 160 fan
Grease and line a 'tray bake style tin' (8 x 12x2in)

Ingredients
200g soft margarine;
150g caster sugar;
250g self-raising flour;
4 eggs;
100g finely chopped walnuts;
2-3 teaspoons instant espresso coffee powder dissolved in 3 teaspoons of hot water from the kettle

Topping
100g icing sugar;
1-2 teaspoons instant espresso coffee powder dissolved in 2 – 3 teaspoons hot water from the kettle;
12 half walnuts to decorate

Method
Place the margarine, sugar, eggs, flour and dissolved coffee into a large mixing bowl and beat using a wooden spoon.

If your margarine is soft this will be easier.

Once combined, continue to beat for at least two minutes. Do not use a mixer, overmixing can cause the top of the finished cake to

Harrogate Coffee and Walnut Cake

appear flaky. When the mixture is fully combined fold in the finely chopped walnuts.

Spoon the mixture into the prepared tin, level the top and bake in the pre-heated oven for 25-30 minutes until it springs back when touched and the middle no longer wobbles.

Test the cake with a skewer and if it comes out clean when pushed gently into the middle, the cake is done.

While the cake is baking, make the icing by placing the dissolved coffee in the bottom of a bowl and adding the icing sugar.

Mix with a knife, this may be trial and error you may need a touch more water if the mixture is too stiff, if so add a teaspoon at a time.

If the mixture is too runny add a little more icing sugar, the finished icing should run off the knife but leave a trail that melts away slowly.

Turn the cake out onto a wire rack and cool.

If the icing has set before the cake has cooled dab your knife into hot water and mix the icing this should be enough to melt the icing again, if it doesn't use another knife end of hot water.

Place the cake right side up (the flattest side) and gently spread the top with the coffee icing.

Arrange walnut halves in rows, each should be about the centre of your cut serving square of cake.

There is sufficient to cut each half walnut in half again and make 24 smaller squares.

This does not make the portion look too small as the cake is quite deep.

'LITTLE SISTERS' CHERRY AND WALNUT COOKIES

I owe such a debt of gratitude to this amazing and dedicated group of people.

Based in Leeds, Mount St Josephs at The Little Sisters of the Poor, work tirelessly to care for the elderly and their outreach work supports the poor and the homeless of our cities.

Along with the nuns there are a team of men and women who provide care and love to all those they come across.

The Little Sisters of the Poor truly embrace faith and family.

Alison Bedford is one such lady. It was she who gave me this recipe.

Please feel free to swap the cherries and the nuts for other ingredients such as apricots and almonds, chocolate chips and more chocolate chips....

Pre-heated oven: Gas 4, 350f, 180c, 160 fan

Ingredients
100g butter;
50g caster sugar;
100g plain flour;
50g glace cherries (chopped or at least halved);
50g chopped walnuts

Method
Cream butter and sugar until light and fluffy, add in the plain flour, mix well until combined.

Fold in the cherries and walnuts. Spoon the mixture onto a baking sheet leaving a space between each biscuit.

Bake for 12-15 minutes until just turning a light golden colour.

'Little Sisters' Cherry
and Walnut Cookies

NHS SHORTBREAD

We are blessed in the north to have some of the most outstanding hospitals in the country; Leeds Teaching Hospital Trust, Bradford Hospital Trust, Liverpool, Sheffield, Manchester, Newcastle the list goes on.

As a nation, we have always valued our NHS, never more so than in 2020 with their absolutely selfless efforts when hit with the coronavirus pandemic.

One of the essential drugs used is morphine, which comes from the milky latex extracted from the seed heads of poppies.

The same effects can't be obtained from a shortbread biscuit with poppy seeds, but I wanted to name a recipe after an organisation I am so proud of.

The secret to good shortbread biscuits is two fold; exact quantities and patience.

I like to make these biscuits with some of them cut out very small so that they are like the little treat you get on the side of your saucer in an up market coffee shop.

Pre-heated oven: Gas 3, 325f, 170c, 150 fan

Ingredients
150g plain flour;
100g cold chopped butter (must be butter);
50g caster sugar;
zest of 2 lemons;
1 teaspoon of poppy seeds

Method
Place the flour, sugar and butter in a bowl and rub together using your fingertips.

When the mixture resembles fine breadcrumbs put in the lemon zest and poppy seeds.

Using the whole of your hand start to work the

133

mixture, this is where patience is needed, squeezing until it all comes together in a ball. Tip onto a lightly floured surface and continue to work together.

Either roll the dough into a sausage shape and chill. Alternatively roll out and cut out biscuits (the size you want) place on a baking tray and chill.

Once the mixture has chilled for between 30 minutes to an hour, remove and bake for 15-20 minutes depending on the size of your biscuit.

For the log of biscuit mixture, cut slices using a sharp knife to the thickness of 1cm lay on a baking sheet and bake as above.

The biscuits need to be cooked but not over coloured.

NHS Shortbread

OTLEY SALAMI

In Otley, West Yorkshire, a Prisoner of War camp was set up around 1944, and the security was rather lax.

Prisoners could be signed out as long as the person doing so was English. The prisoners were able to work in the local train stations of Bingley and Keighley unloading goods.

Many of them remained at the camp until well after the war, often due to having nowhere to go.

Many made their home in the area and settled down to a life in the north. Salami would have been a common food among them – but perhaps not a chocolate one! And what a special treat you end up with.

I make this for Christmas to give as a gift, its fabulous served after dinner.

Ingredients
50g flaked almonds, or chopped hazelnuts;
150g amaretti biscuits (crushed);
200g dark chocolate (the darker the better);
150g unsalted butter;
3 tablespoons brandy (or another sprit) – I like to use Amaretto liqueur;
25g ground almonds;
1 tablespoon icing sugar

Method
Toast the almonds or hazelnuts by spreading onto a baking sheet and placing in a hot oven about 180c, gas 6 for 2-3 minutes.

Take out and turn using a spatula and bake again.

I tend to use flaked almonds and I like to toast them till very dark (somewhat like burnt almonds).

Remove when the nuts are the colour you want.

Crush the amaretti biscuits finely either using a

Otley Salami

processor (be careful this could make them too fine) or use a plastic bag and rolling pin.

If you can't get the amaretti biscuits, you could use a plain rich tea biscuit.

Melt the chocolate, butter and brandy in a bowl set over a pan of barely simmering water.

When melted tip in the nuts, ground almonds and the crushed biscuits. Place the bowl of dough in the fridge to firm up about two hours.

When the mixture has chilled, tip out onto a sheet of cling film, using the film and your hands roll and mould the mixture into a salami shape.

Chill until firm then roll the 'salami' in the icing sugar, this gives that real authentic look.

I have doubled the quantities and made several smaller salamis wrapped in waxed paper tied with string and given as a gift and also used hazelnut liquor.

Chopped dried cherries, walnuts, white chocolate chips also work in place of the nuts.

SLY CAKE DATE PASTRY

When food is wrapped in pastry it always seems to have that northern feel.

I take my hat off to the folk of Cornwall for their delicious pasty and to other southern counties that make pies both sweet and savory.

But here in the north we are so apt at wrapping most things in pastry and giving it a fancy name. Most of the time we are trying to use up leftovers or covering over a culinary disaster (or is that just me?)

Sly cake, so called because on the surface the dish looks like a sheet of cooked pastry but 'slyly' inside sits a sticky treat of fruit and nuts.

Part 4

This pastry recipe is delicious and versatile.

If you make it with self-raising flour it becomes light and cake-like, however, if you make it with plain flour it is crisp and perfect for sweet tart cases like a lemon meringue pie or fruit tartlet.

The great thing about this pastry is that it has little shrinkage when baked.

This 'pasty pastry' can also be filled with currants, sweet mincemeat, stewed apple, jam and cinnamon or with walnuts scattered.

Ingredients
500g self-raising flour;
200g soft butter;
100g icing sugar;
2 medium eggs;
500g chopped stoned dates;
300mls water;
¼ teaspoon bicarbonate of soda (no more);
1 egg yolk beaten to glaze (milk can be an alternative);
1 tablespoon of granulated or nibbed sugar
Pre-heated oven: Gas 4, 350f, 180c, 160 fan

Method
Cream the butter and sugar until light and fluffy, add in the beaten egg and mix well.

Gently mix in the flour, and using your hands bring together to form a ball, wrap and chill for at least two hours.

Put the chopped dates and water into a pan, bring the mixture to a boil and reduce the heat to a simmer.

Allow the dates to soften, stirring occasionally.

Watch the mixture as the water can soon evaporate and the dates stick to the pan. If the dates are not softening, then add a little more water but no more than 50mls at a time extra.

A lot of this process will depend on how dry the dates are.

If you are using fresh or 'eating' dates, the 300mls of water will be sufficient.

If you are using a block of dried dates you may need to add a little more.

Once the dates are soft and while the mixture is hot,

Sly Cake Date Pastry

add the bicarbonate of soda (dissolved in a teaspoon of cold water).

The mixture will foam up and that helps to make the date filling soft and spreadable.

Use an 8 x 12 x 2in cake pan (this makes a good deep pasty and the dates don't spill out) if you are making it with jam then a Swiss roll tin is perfect, the rule being the softer the filling the deeper the cake tin.

Roll out half of the pastry and use to line the base and sides of the cake tin, it is very forgiving and can be 'patched' up if it should break.

Because this pastry is soft, I tend to roll it out between two sheets of greaseproof paper.

Spread the cooled filling over the base, roll out the top half of the pastry, try to keep this top as neat and possible as it's on show.

Press the edges together as best as you can, it needs the filling to be encased.

Glaze the top with beaten egg yolk or milk, sprinkle with sugar and bake for about 35–40 minutes until golden and crisp on top.

Leave to cool in the tin for about 20 minutes to completely firm up, then gently turn out allow to cool completely before cutting into bars.

SOLDIERS CRISP

This recipe calls for invalid toffee, not a name used much these days, but amongst the convalescing soldiers it was an extremely popular sweet treat, thus giving it the name.

Many were recuperating in one of the 3,000 or more auxiliary hospitals set up during the First World War.

They were managed by the British Red Cross and the St Johns of Jerusalem organisations forming a Joint War Committee.

Soldiers Crisp

Large houses, stately homes, town halls and church halls were converted, with women from the local community working voluntarily and part time to help nurse the wounded service men.

Local medics would also volunteer despite the heavy workload of the general hospitals.

The north of England, including, Leicestershire, Lincolnshire, Cheshire, Lancashire, Yorkshire (all ridings), Durham, Northumberland, Cumberland and Westmorland housed 500 or so auxiliary hospitals.

Other toffees can be used if you can't find the original creamy one.

Ingredients
150g creamy toffees;
100g butter;
150g marshmallows;

200g Rice Krispies (a few less if you like it stickier)

Method
In a large pan melt the toffees, marshmallows, and butter very slowly, stirring frequently. The toffees are usually the last to melt.

Please don't be tempted to turn the heat up because the toffees won't melt any quicker but you will burn the marshmallows.

When all the ingredients have melted, give the

mixture a good stir until it is all well amalgamated.

Take the pan off the heat and tip in the Rice Krispies, give the mixture a good stir until all are well coated in the sticky goo.

Tip the mixture into a 12 x 8 x 2in cake tin and press down.

If the mixture is hot use the back of a spoon,

however don't worry, it will soon cool down.

Using damp fingers is a good way to give the mixture a good final press until it is even and smooth on top.

Chill until set, and then cut into squares.

Why not try using different flavours of toffee and maybe even add a touch of flaked salt to give it that adult twist?

If this recipe is not decadent enough you could always spread the top with chocolate.

'ONE F'R NOW...
AND ONE F'T SNAP TIN'

A term used to describe 'batch' baking.
Something to eat now, plus some to give away or save for later.
'Tin tin tin' translates as 'It isn't in the tin'.

FLO THOMPSON'S GROUND RICE TARTS

HOLLYWOOD CHOCOLATE PASTRY

HUSTLEWAITE CAKE

MANCHESTER LOAF

MOGGY

SANDRA'S FRUIT CAKE

SCARBOROUGH LOAF

MUM'S APRICOT AND BRANDY MINCEMEAT

SPECIAL MINCE PIES

TEMPLE NEWSAM LOAF

THE BEST NORTHERN SHORT CRUST PASTRY

TINNED CARAMEL

YORKSHIRE PALS CAKE - WHITE CHRISTMAS CAKE

Flo Thompson's
Ground Rice Tarts

FLO THOMPSON'S GROUND RICE TARTS

A neighbour of ours who used to bake religiously for the church bazaar gave this recipe to my mum many years before I was born.

She used to say in her Yorkshire dialect, "weight of two eggs in butter, sugar and ground rice, if tha makin' em f't bizaar weight of six eggs."

It took me many years to understand what it actually meant but now I get it.

Weigh the eggs and use this as a measurement for the other ingredients.

It was always a thing in our house to make a 'few ground rice tarts' with any leftover pastry.

I've used ground rice or semolina for these but have even been known to substitute fine polenta, which leaves the tarts quite 'nutty' in texture.

Some may use all ground rice yet I prefer them half rice, semolina or polenta to flour, that makes them a little lighter.

Pre-heated oven: Gas 6, 400f, 200c, 180 fan

You will need a bun tray or 12 whole tart tins

Ingredients
½ batch of 'The Best Northern Short Crust Pastry' (if you are making a lot use the whole batch); 2 large eggs, weigh the cracked eggs and use this amount in the following:

soft butter;
caster sugar;
self-raising flour and ground rice (half of each gives a nice texture);
2 tablespoons of jam or curd (your preference)

Method

Roll out the pastry and cut circles using a biscuit cutter, cut the circle slightly larger than case, this will give a little 'side' to the tarts.

Drop about half a teaspoon of jam or curd in the bottom of each case and set aside.

In a mixing bowl, cream the butter and sugar until light and fluffy. Add the eggs and fold in the ground rice and flour mixture.

I like to add some lemon or orange zest at this point as it gives another dimension.

Using a dessert spoon or large teaspoon, spoon some of this mixture on top of the jam filled pastry cases.

It's a bit of trial and error here to know just how much mixture to use.

It's about not too much so the filling spills out while cooking or putting in too little so they appear somewhat bereft, one rounded dessert spoon usually does it. Bake for about 20–25 minutes until dark golden and the pastry is light brown.

Leave to cool if you can manage it because they are so beautiful eaten slightly warm.

A personal favourite is served as a pudding swimming in evaporated milk (but I wouldn't admit this to anyone!).

HOLLYWOOD CHOCOLATE PASTRY

This gorgeous pastry does not come from Hollywood, USA, but originated in a handshake from the man – Paul Hollywood master baker, TV presenter and *Great British Bake Off* judge.

Paul loved this pastry so much that he gave me the famous gesture. Anyone familiar with *GBBO* will know that when anyone in the tent gets the 'Hollywood handshake' it means spot on.

Hollywood
Chocolate Pastry

His initial words to me were, "That pastry looks a bit thick Sandy, doesn't look crisp buts let's see."

Then there was music as the knife glided down the case emitting the perfect pitch of 'crunch'. He lifted the pastry up to his mouth where it melted on contact. Boom! Perfection, and now you can achieve the same.

This is a rich and crisp and delicious pastry.

Wherever I can I like to double up on how a recipe can be used, and this is no exception.

This can even be used for cutting out biscuits (roll the mixture slightly more, about the thickness of a pound coin) and bake at the same temperature as the pastry.

It is especially fabulous when used with a chocolate tart filling.

Chocolate on chocolate, is there anything better?

Pre-heated oven: Gas 5, 375f, 180c, fan 160c

Ingredients
175gms plain flour;
½ teaspoon baking powder;
50gms cocoa;
50gms icing sugar;
140gms unsalted butter;
3 egg yolks

Method
Mix the flour, sugar, and cocoa in a processor and run for a second or two.

Put the cut butter into the processor and pulse until it resembles fine breadcrumbs.

Drop in the egg yolks and mix for a few seconds.

Tip onto a surface and bring the dough together with your hand. Wrap the ball in cling film and chill.

Roll dough between two sheets of cling film and use to line tart tin or for biscuits.

HUSTLEWAITE CAKE

Known historically as 'The orchard village of the north' due to its loamy soil and micro-climate, Hustlewaite was able to compete with the fruit growers of the south with crops such as vines and apricots.

Most of the cottages in the village were growing one kind of fruit crop or another and in the heydays of the village, these luscious fruits were shipped by rail to places such a Hartlepool to make jam.

During the 1960s, the train station was closed and slowly the orchards disappeared. Nevertheless, following the publication of a book in 2009 depicting the village's history, a new generation of volunteers planted over 1,000 trees, mainly rare apple varieties.

Then came the cider mill, which put to excellent use any leftover apples.

A gorgeous cake that really needs no decorating as the flavours are contained within, I made this for my very first challenge on *Bake Off* and it has been a firm favourite ever since.

I have been known to take the odd short cut when baking which often leads to a disaster. While preparing for *Bake Off*, my sister reminded me to always line my baking tin (I often believed that a good greasing would suffice).

On the show, I was asked what was I doing, as I meticulously lined it.

"My sisters last words to me were 'don't forget to line your tin'," I said nervously.

Once the programme went live, I was inundated with words of condolence and could not understand what was happening.

Suddenly the penny dropped. My sister's last words!! I hurriedly went on social media to say they were her last words to me as I left for the tent. Oops.

Hustlewaite Cake

This is a lovely cake to give as a gift, I baked one using a different tin when I was asked to mark the 200th birthday for Anne Bronte by the Bronte Society. I'm always delighted to support Yorkshire Heritage.

Pre-heated oven: Gas 3, 325f, 170c, 150 fan
Grease and line a 2lb loaf tin.

Ingredients
250g soft butter (always use butter, preferably unsalted);
200g caster sugar;
200g self-raising flour;
100g plain flour;
3 large eggs;
200g chopped apricots;
150mls almond liquor

Method
Put the chopped apricots and liquor in a small pan and warm under a very low light. The alcohol will come to the boil quickly; you don't want the liquid to evaporate.

Once the mixture has boiled turn off the heat and leave to stand so the apricots soak up the almond liquor.

Cream together the butter and sugar until light and fluffy. Add the eggs and mix well. While adding the eggs, stir in the combined flours and mix until you have a firm cake batter.

Stir in the soaked apricots and any liquid (there should be little as apricots soak up the liquor). Mix well until all the chopped apricots are evenly distributed.

Spoon the mixture into the prepared cake tin and smooth out the top.

Bake the cake on the middle shelf for 1-1½ hours until the top has domed in the middle and the classic crack has appeared. Double check the cake by pushing a thin sharp knife down the centre. If it comes out clean then the cake is cooked.

If the top looks to be getting too brown and the centre is not cooked it may be that your oven is too hot.

Ovens differ, you know your own oven. Bake this on the cooler side of the setting rather than the hotter.

Part 5

MANCHESTER LOAF

In 1890, a Scotsman called Montgomerie came up with an idea to warm dough with malt to a temperature where the enzymes broke down the starch in the dough, converting some to maltose.

Circa 1920, Mr Sorensen and Mr Green created a malt loaf 'Soreen', produced in Manchester and still made there today. I'm sure my Lancashire cousins won't mind advocating Yorkshire Tea in this recipe.

Malt bread is underrated. I won't knock the bought variety, but try making some and you'll be pleasantly surprised, but do leave it wrapped for two days.

Pre-heated oven: Gas 2, 200f, 150c, 130 fan
Grease and line 2 x 1lb loaf tins

Ingredients
150mls very strong black tea (use any brand as long as its Yorkshire Tea!!);
175g malt extract;
100g molasses sugar;
300g raisins;
2 eggs beaten;
250g self-raising flour;
½ teaspoon of bicarbonate of soda

Method
Mix the hot tea and malt extract in a bowl, add sugar and dried fruit, stir well and leave to cool allowing the fruit to 'plump up'.

Stir again when cool and add in the beaten eggs. Tip in the flour and bicarb and working quickly divide the mixture between the tins. Bake for approximately 50 minutes until well risen and firm to the touch. While still hot, brush the top with a little malt extract to glaze.

Turn out and leave to cool completely before wrapping in greaseproof paper and foil. Store for at least a good day longer if you can wait that long. Slice and serve with lashings of butter.

Manchester Loaf

Moggy

MOGGY

Old Norse for Mugi, meaning corn or flour, Moggy is made in many regions of Yorkshire.

Textile, coalmining and steel working communities all made their own version, most commonly a ginger sponge and as we say in the north 'using treacle'.

That more often meant 'golden syrup' but dark rich black treacle was also used.

Moggy was always made in a roasting tin or dripping tin and presented as a slab cake, usually sunken in the middle.

This cake has been handed down over generations and works every time.

It is gorgeous with a drizzle of lemon icing over the top or the zest of an orange in the mix.

It is magical with custard, but best of all served with a cup of tea, it just makes the world a better place.

I have, on occasion, used wholemeal, self-raising flour which gives a more robust texture and slightly more 'parkin' feel to the cake.
Pre-heated oven: Gas 4, 350f, 180c, 160 fan

Ingredients
450g self-raising flour;
150g sugar;
150g margarine;
3 tablespoons golden syrup or black treacle;
200mls boiled water;
2 eggs;
3–5 teaspoons ground ginger (depending on taste);
1 good teaspoon bicarbonate of soda

Method
Grease and line a deep oblong tin 12in x 9in, a 9in round cake tin, or split the mixture between two deep 7in tins (whichever you use it needs to be deep as the cake has a good rise).

Melt the margarine, sugar and syrup in a saucepan over a low heat.

In a large mixing bowl

mix together the flour, bicarb and ground ginger.

When the margarine has melted, pour over the flour etc. and mix until well combined. Beat into the mixture the 2 eggs until well incorporated.

With the water just off the boil, carefully pour the into the mixture and stir well.

This will make the mixture look terrible but trust me keep going, when

you have a smooth foamy batter pour into the greased lined tin.

Bake for about an hour until the cake is firm to the touch and a knife comes out clean when inserted into the centre.

Cool in the tin for 10 minutes then turn out onto a wire rack. This cake keeps for up to a week if stored in a tin and actually improves as the week passes.

SANDRA'S FRUIT CAKE

Here is a fabulous fruit cake recipe. Sandra, a very good friend of mine, gave it me.

She lives in Burn Bridge near Harrogate and it was given to her by her friend from Cleckheaton and so as with all good recipes the handing down goes on and on through generations.

Please feel free to chop and change this recipe, add whatever fruit combinations you prefer just make sure it adds up to the 1,500gm.

This makes three 2lb cakes which is great for sharing or six 1lb loaf cakes, perfect for giving away.

It's lighter than a Christmas cake but it would make a great substitute for any richer offering.

Pre-heated oven: Gas 2, 200f, 150c, 130 fan
Grease and line 3 x 2lb loaf tins or two 8in round cake tins.

Sandra's Fruit Cake

Ingredients
1kg dried mixed fruit;
500g glace cherries (whole
halved or chopped which
ever you prefer);
1 large tin of crushed
pineapple;
300gm soft brown sugar;
200gms butter;
4 beaten eggs;
500g self-raising flour;
1 level teaspoon of baking
powder

Method
Put the fruit, cherries, sugar,
pineapple plus juice and the
butter into a large pan.
Heat gently until it boils
and leave to cool before
adding the eggs, flour and
baking powder.
Divide the mixture
between cake tins, level the
top and bake for 1 hour and
15 minutes until dark
golden brown and a skewer
comes out clean when
inserted into the middle.

Optional: before removing cake from tin pierce several times
with a skewer and spoon over some brandy.

SCARBOROUGH LOAF

This loaf is fabulous when
you want to make a few or a
large batch for the kind of
person who bakes for fetes,
fairs or bazaars. One of the
oldest and largest fairs was
Scarborough Fair.

It was originally a 45 day
trading event and given a
Royal Charter in 1253 by
King Henry III.

Such was its reputation,
traders from Europe would
attend and it attracted food
sellers and entertainers who
cashed in on the masses.

The event was captured
in a folk song written
around 1670, which later
became a chart hit record by
Simon and Garfunkel.

When I was a child, I'd
watch my mum make these
cakes and used to call them

datenut walnut cakes and the name stuck. Mum would often double the recipe and make about six 1lb loaf tins, in most cases for the school fair. They would be wrapped and needed no decorations just a pack of best butter.

Dad would watch her make these cakes, usually drooling, but unable to get his hands on them.

One day he asked her how much would she get for such a cake at the school fair? She told him and he put in his hand in his pocket and bought one.

Could we get a piece off him? No chance, but he did sell us a slice!

Yorkshireman to the core was our dad.

This recipe makes three cakes; one for now, another for later and one to give away.

Pre-heated oven: Gas 3, 325f, 170c, 150 fan
Grease and line 3 x 1lb loaf tins.

Ingredients
600g self-raising flour;
200g sugar (100g white sugar, 100g brown sugar);
500g chopped dried dates;
150g chopped walnuts;
100g margarine;
400ml boiling water;
1 teaspoon bicarbonate of soda (dissolved in 1 tablespoon milk);
2 beaten eggs

Method
Pour boiling water over the chopped dates and margarine, stir and leave to cool. Stir in the sugar, flour and chopped walnuts, then add the beaten eggs.

Make sure this mixture is all well amalgamated before adding the dissolved bicarb.

Mix well!

Fill the lined loaf tins up to half way and bake in a slow oven for 45 minutes to an hour. The cakes should be well risen and dark golden brown.

When a skewer is inserted in the middle it should come out clean, if it

Scarborough Loaf

doesn't leave the cake a little longer with the oven turned down a touch so the top does not burn. When the cooked cakes have set for a minute or two in the tin turn out onto a wire rack and allow to cool completely.

Wrap the loaf cakes in cling film and ideally store for a day to improve the flavour.

Spread a cut slice generously with best salted butter (preferably Yorkshire Dales butter).

MUM'S APRICOT AND BRANDY MINCEMEAT

You are very privileged to be getting this recipe. Christmas is not Christmas without Shelia's mincemeat.

It is now left to my sister and I to carry on this tradition and we would like to share it with you.

Ingredients
200g dried chopped apricots (chop finely);
4 limes;
1kg mixture of currants, sultanas and raisins;
4 tablespoons lime marmalade;
500g demerara sugar;
200g suet – I use veggie;
2 teaspoons ground mixed spice;
300ml brandy

Method
Grate the rind of the limes, strain the juice. Mix with the apricots, dried fruit, marmalade, sugar, suet and spice. Cover and leave to stand for 24 hours.

Stir in the brandy then fill jars right to the top. Keep them in a cool place for up to six months. Add a little more brandy and you're good to go.

This mixture can be frozen, however, leave the mixture to stand for a month after making before freezing.

When you are ready to make pies defrost and leave to stand overnight before using.

Sheila's sweet mince meat

SPECIAL MINCE PIES

Perfect for mum's sweet mincemeat but also try using this pastry and some bought mincemeat.

This is a different pastry, a cross between pastry and cake, it has a crisp outer shell which reveals a light cakey inside. It's ideal not just for Christmas mince pies but any other fruit pies all year round.

The great thing about this pastry is that it raises slightly while baking and moulds around the filling, preventing 'boiling out 'that can sometimes happen.

I usually make a batch in the food processor, but it can be made by hand it just takes quite a bit longer to work in the egg. The first rolling can be crumbly but please bear with it, it loves to be rolled and re-rolled, which cannot always be said for short crust pastry.

Pre-heated oven: Gas 6, 400f, 200c, 180 fan

Ingredients
500g self-raising flour;
pinch of salt;
200g granulated sugar;
250g block of margarine (must be margarine and must be block);
1 egg;
a little milk to seal the pies;
pinch of granulated sugar on the top (optional)

Method
In the bowl of a large food processor tip in the flour and pinch of salt.

Cut the block of cold margarine into small pieces and drop them in. Let the machine run until the mix resembles fine breadcrumbs.

If you don't have a processor, use a spacious bowl and rub the margarine into the flour.

Add the sugar and give the mixture a quick wiz or stir. Crack the egg into the flour and sugar mixture and keep the processor going, it may appear that the egg is not enough to bind the mixture but hold tight it will manage it. If you are doing this by hand, just be patient and work the dough with your hands and it will eventually come together.

When the dough has come together, tip out the mixture onto a floured surface and knead until smooth.

There is no need to chill this pastry it can be used immediately if required.

This recipe makes a large amount of pastry and will make at least three dozen mince pies.

The cooked pies will keep without freezing for a week, but they will also freeze very well.

Roll out the pastry using the same size cutter for the top and bottom cut out all the discs you need depending on how much mincemeat you have. Press a disc of pastry into the bottom of the tart tray. This pastry is very forgiving and will mould easily.

Fill the tart case with a good, heaped teaspoon of sweet mincemeat and using a second disc with the underside brushed with a little milk pop it over the mincemeat.

Press the edges together, and sprinkle the top with a little sugar.

Snip three holes using the tip of some scissors (my grandma said these were to represent the Three Wise Men who came to the Christmas Nativity).

Bake for about 20 to 30 minutes depending on how dark you like your pastry.

The longer you bake them the crisper they are. A more lightly golden bake results in a cakier finish.

Special mince pies

TEMPLE NEWSAM LOAF

The first recorded cup of tea, then called 'China drink' was around 1660, written in the Samuel Pepys diaries.

However in 1644, in the grand stately home of Temple Newsam, lived landowner and politician Sir Arthur Ingram, who was ordering tea or some kind of 'China drink' by the bottle.

It is not quite certain if he just loved the new drink or because someone in the household may have been quite ill, as tea was drunk as a nurturing medicine.

As a child I wasn't quite sure if this cake was eaten while drinking tea, had to be eaten for tea, was made in a 'T' shape or there was tea in it.

Some people butter this moist delicious loaf, but it is equally fabulous with or without.

Please feel free to swap and change the tea you use.

I use Taylors of Harrogate and also prefer to use one type of dried fruit, but mixed fruit can be equally as good.

Pre-heated oven: Gas 2, 200f, 150c, 130 fan
Grease and line a 2lb loaf tin or two 1lb loaf tins

Ingredients
300g sultanas;
100g soft brown sugar;
400ml freshly brewed tea – I use two Earl Grey (whichever tea you use it needs to be quite strong);
2 beaten eggs;
1 teaspoon of mixed spice;
juice and zest of 1 large orange;
300g self-raising wholemeal flour;
glaze;
1 tablespoon of sugar;
2 tablespoons of milk

Temple Newsam Loaf

Method

Make up the tea. While still hot add the fruit, juice and zested orange and soak (preferably overnight).

If you can't wait then pour the brewed tea (without the bag) and fruit into a pan and warm, this speeds up the soaking process.

Once cooled add the sugar, eggs, spices and flour mix until combined.

If the mixture is too stiff (some of the liquid could have evaporated if you used the warming method) add a drop of tea or orange juice. Pour the mixture into the greased and lined tin or tins, level the top.

Bake in the pre-heated oven for 1½ hours or until a skewer inserted in the middle comes out clean. Cool on a wire rack.

For the glaze, heat the milk and the sugar until boiling, allow to boil for about a minute and then brush onto the cooked cake while it is still warm. This cake will keep for a week wrapped in an air-tight tin.

169

Best Northern
Short Crust Pastry Ever

BEST NORTHERN SHORT CRUST PASTRY EVER

This fits all short crust pastry needs. I make it all the time for anything sweet or savoury that requires a short crust.

It was taught to me by my mum who stressed that any great cooking starts with good pastry.

Whether you need this entire amount or not, it's worth making a batch and freezing the rest.

No matter how much, though, the rule is half fats to flour.

I always use self-raising flour for a lighter texture and a spoonful of icing sugar to stabilize, even if it's for a savoury dish, hence the 'one size fits all.'

Ingredients
500g self-raising flour;
125g block margarine;
125g lard or vegetable white fat;
1 teaspoon of salt;
1 tablespoon icing sugar;
cold water

Method
Sift the flour, salt and icing sugar into a bowl. Cut the fats into small cubes and rub into flour with fingertips.

Combine mixture until it resembles fine breadcrumbs. Keep agitating the bowl and bigger lumps will rise.

It will depend on the porousness of the flour as to how much water is needed. Add only a bit at a time as you don't want it to become too sticky and tough.

Using a table knife, work 2–3 tablespoons of water in until you have a firm dough or the pastry won't roll out. Trial and error, you'll master the feel of the perfect result.

One secret to perfect pastry is resting. Wrap the dough in foil, cling film or greaseproof paper and chill for 30 minutes. If you have time, up to an hour is best.

Take out about 15-30 minutes before needed to bring up to temperature and allow for good rolling.

TINNED CARAMEL

Here's a cheeky idea. Anyone who remembers the late, fabulous Gary Rhodes will recall how he boiled an unopen tin of condensed milk for about two hours to get a lovely rich caramel.

Then the shops started to sell condensed milk already caramelised.

I've gone one further and, in true northern tradition, at a fraction of the cost and produced something so much richer and darker in colour and flavour.

Once boiled, the caramel will keep to the date printed on the tin.

Fill the slow cooker with tins of unopened condensed milk, cover the whole lot with boiling water making sure that the tins are completely covered, put the slow cooker on low and leave overnight.

That's basically it.

Remove the tins and cool, keep them in the fridge and label up, you now have a ready dessert.

Use in the ice cream recipe here in place of the normal condensed milk, mix into butter cream for a sumptuous taste, or sandwich a chocolate cake with this butter cream for a 'Rolo cake'.

Spread on the bottom of a pastry case, top with sliced bananas and whipped cream for a quick banoffee pie or even spread between cookies for that extra special sandwich biscuit.

Tip: the longer you leave it the darker it gets to the point where it can be sliced but never let the water run dry – I speak from experience!

Tinned caramel

Yorkshire Pals Cake

YORKSHIRE PALS CAKE – WHITE CHRISTMAS CAKE

Christmas Eve, 1914.

Four months into the First World War, and a group of Yorkshire soldiers referred to as the Yorkshire Pals sat in the trenches thinking of home.

Suddenly the rain stopped, the skies cleared and the gun fire ceased. Both British and German troops lay down their weapons and called a truce for Christmas.

Carols were sung and they played a game of football, gifts of chocolate and cigarettes were shared, the hand of goodwill was extended along with food.

It would be heart-warming to think that some of the Yorkshire Pals had been sent "a bit 'o'cake" from home to offer.

This Cake is in memory of all the men who gave their lives in conflict.

Not that it is just for Christmas. Far from it.

It's an alternative to a rich dark fruit cake, perfect for someone who prefers glace fruit rather than dried mixed fruit.

I've used combinations of different glace fruits in this cake as so much depends on what is available.

I am fortunate to have been able to buy some fabulous glace fruit from the 'The Nut shop' in Leeds Kirkgate Market.

Try adding some sliced toasted almonds into the mix.

Finally, it goes without saying that a healthy slice of cheese is the desirable accompaniment.

Pre-heated oven: Gas 3, 325f, 170c, 150 fan
Grease and line an 8in round cake tin or 7in square.

Ingredients

200g soft margarine or butter;

200g caster sugar;

4 eggs;

50g ground rice / fine polenta;

100g ground almonds;

225g of glace fruit and nuts, the choice is yours: cherries, glace pineapple, oranges, apricots, pear etc;

sliced toasted almonds;

chopped toasted hazelnuts;

chopped walnuts;

100g self-raising flour;

1 teaspoon of vanilla extract

Method

Cream the butter or margarine with the sugar until light and fluffy, mix in the vanilla extract.

Chop the fruit finely (I often use scissors).

If there is rather a lot of syrup, wash them, place the chopped fruit in a sieve and run it under the cold tap then pat dry.

When the chopped fruit is dried mix it with the nuts, flour, ground almonds and ground rice / polenta.

Add half of the beaten egg to the creamed butter and sugar, mix well, add a few tablespoons of the fruit and flour mixture and keep mixing, add the rest of the egg and the fruit, nut and flour mixture.

Give the mixture a good stir until the fruit and nuts are evenly distributed.

Tip the mixture into the prepared tin, level the top and bake for approximately 1¼ hours or until a skewer inserted in the middle comes out clean.

Leave in the tin for 10 minutes before turning out to cool completely.

Beautiful!

Investigate our other titles and
stay up to date with all our latest releases at
www.scratchingshedpublishing.co.uk